DON'T
RUN
OUT OF
MONEY!

- A Shot Across the Bow -

By Bob Hydeman

Don't Run Out of Money! A Shot Across the Bow

mbsmith@parkcitiespublishing.com

Mary Beth Smith

Park Cities Publishing

CONTENTS

FOREWORD

In the Navy, a shot across the bow is a warning to be taken very seriously. If you want to keep your own ship afloat throughout your life, Bob Hydeman's book, "Don't Run Out of Money! A Shot Across the Bow" needs to be taken equally seriously!

History not only repeats itself, but it establishes recognizable trends that explain and predict the future. This book identifies those trends that threaten your ability to take care of yourself past retirement age. Bob encourages the reader to recognize and get ahead of the trends rather than be blindsided.

The future gets here very quickly and "Don't Run Out of Money! A Shot Across the Bow" makes you aware of the importance of managing your financial health.

Forewarned is forearmed!

Roger Staubach
Dallas, TX
May 2017

INTRODUCTION

"Don't Run Out of Money! A Shot Across the Bow" is intended to be practical American history - a history that helps the reader understand how things have evolved from what they were over a hundred years ago to what they are today.

I've recorded real, personal history as experienced by my father and me. Sharing it allows the reader to follow economic trends that can be projected into the future, and the reader will have the best possible insight as to what to expect, and what needs to be prepared for during the rest of his or her life through retirement.

This book is not an ego trip. I didn't write it to promote either my father or myself. The inspiration behind writing is sincere. I am deeply concerned about the future that my kids and grandkids and their families, and the families of my countrymen, and my country itself will be challenged by in the immediate future and forever.

My writing is not about HOW to do anything. Instead, it explains WHY you have to do, and WHAT you have to do in order to survive and thrive financially throughout your lifetime.

Politicians have the power to set the tone in our country, and unfortunately, they tell us what they want us to hear and believe, not what is really the truth. Politicians on both sides of the aisle refuse to tell us the truth about our nation because the truth won't get them elected or reelected. Politicians who are in office, in order to keep their seats in office, tell us what a great job they are doing for us, and they make promises foretelling what they are going to keep doing for us. They use numbers, with a spin that favors them, to prove their points.

Using those numbers as proof, they then make promises that they can't possibly keep. Politicians who are trying to replace an incumbent use their own spin on the numbers to show the voter that the incumbent is doing a lousy job and needs to be replaced. He or she then makes promises that can't possibly be kept in order to gain votes, and win the seat.

I call these promises 'happy talk'. I've created a new word to describe this happy talk, EBSA, which is an acronym of the phrase Enough Bull Strudel Already! Unfortunately, the American people are being fed a lot of bull strudel. There is no bull strudel in this book. It is an accurate history with real numbers that can be authenticated, and these numbers follow accurate, chronological trends. (I am not running for office, and that is my only political promise.)

As you read, don't think about my father or me; Think of how what you are reading pertains to the future of your family and yourself.

My hope is that this book will help its readers recognize the distinction between happy talk and the truth so that they can clearly see and prepare for the huge challenges that lie ahead. The truth can be hard to swallow, but being aware of it and preparing for it is far better than being blindsided by it.

Believing happy talk can lead to disaster. Don't count on political promises that can't be kept. Count on yourself and common sense to adjust to the changes that are inevitable based on the four unstoppable trends - The Big Four - that are depicted in this book.

Real numbers don't lie!!

EBSA!

PART I

A TWENTIETH CENTURY TALE

Chapter 1

MY DAD AND THE PURCHASING POWER OF A DOLLAR
1913-1960

The American dream includes the ability to retire comfortably at an age young enough to be able to enjoy retirement. This dream has been a reality for millions of Americans for as long as most of us can remember. Shockingly, this dream is fading fast or has already faded for those of us who are not independently wealthy.

I am writing this book from a somewhat unique perspective: I was born in 1936 to a father who was born in 1895.

I now have 80 years of personal history, but I also have the advantage of knowing about my father's experiences, giving me a firsthand look at the cost of living going back over 120 years. Our combined histories are pertinent to every American because they depict a verifiable historical financial trend that will be accelerating and will influence everyone's long term financial future.

My Dad

In 1895, Sid L. Hydeman was born into a wealthy York, Pennsylvania family that owned several sizeable department stores in major and secondary cities. He was the oldest of three sons and in line to run the family business. The family wanted him to go to the Wharton School of Business at the University of Pennsylvania, but my father had other career plans. In 1913, at the age of 18, he ran away from home to pursue his dream of becoming an artist in New York City.

At this time, gold was valued at $20.67 an ounce.

Dad's two younger brothers, my uncles, went on to attend business school at Penn, inherited the family business, and became quite wealthy. In the meanwhile, my father was a struggling artist in the big city, and living on fumes. He had a roommate by the name of Hoagy Carmichael, who was a struggling song writer.

Hoagy became a very successful and famous composer, pianist, singer, actor and bandleader. He is best known for composing four of the most recorded American songs of all time, "Stardust," "Georgia on My Mind," "The Nearness of You," and "Heart and Soul."

Hoagy and my father shared the rent on their apartment in New York City, which was a stretch for them at $5.00 a month. $2.50 each. Think about that! It was costing my father and Hoagy about 8 cents each a day for their apartment rent. The landlord was charging Hoagy and my father 16 cents a day, and he was making a satisfactory profit on that basis on a rental property in Manhattan in New York City! I was in the grocery store today and saw that regular sized candy bars are selling for $1.59. Back then, $1.59 would have paid for almost twenty days of my father's monthly rent!

The penny used to have value!

Hoagy and my father used to eat lunch for a nickel. This included two hotdogs at two cents apiece, and a lemonade for a penny. They ate like this regularly.

My father was an outstanding commercial and graphic artist. One of his specialties was pen and ink portrait art, at which he was exceptional. Because he had a great sense of humor, he was also a cartoonist. His cartoon, which was nationally syndicated in newspapers across the country, was about two sailors named "Salt and Pepper."

George Washington Pen and Ink by My Father

SID HYDEMAN FINDS SUCCESS

Pop's talent brought him honors, connections and financial success. He worked both for magazines and newspapers and became, at different times, the art editor of major magazines such as Cosmopolitan, Harper's Bazaar, Red Book, and Liberty. He was considered one of the deans of art editors for magazines in the big city of New York.

During these exciting years, my father met and became good friends with Walt Disney. When I was born, Walt graciously accepted his request to be my Godfather. I was too young to remember meeting Walt, but he never forgot my birthday or Christmas. I had original, signed Disney art all over my bedroom.

I have a letter inviting my father to become a member of the Artist and Writer's Golf Association. The invitation was extended in September of 1928. At this time, this invitation was considered to be a high honor, offered to only the most successful in my father's field. The invitation came with a price. The membership dues were $15.00 a year, which included greens fees, dinners and prizes for both the fall and the spring one day tournaments.

Pop met and instantly fell head-over-heels for a beautiful model and aspiring actress, Miriam Breschel, from Rye, NY. She was 21 years younger than he was when they married in 1935. I came along the next year. By this time my father was almost 42 and extremely successful. We lived at 1088 Park Avenue. Our apartment, which also housed the live-in servants, became too small with my arrival. My father had a butler/chauffeur, my mother had a maid/cleaning lady, and I had a nanny. We took and needed a whole floor apartment at 565 Park Avenue. Amazingly, the rent in both places was the same: $300.00 a month. By comparison, 1088 Park Avenue is now a co-op building, and apartments sell for over $3,000,000.00. An apartment comparable

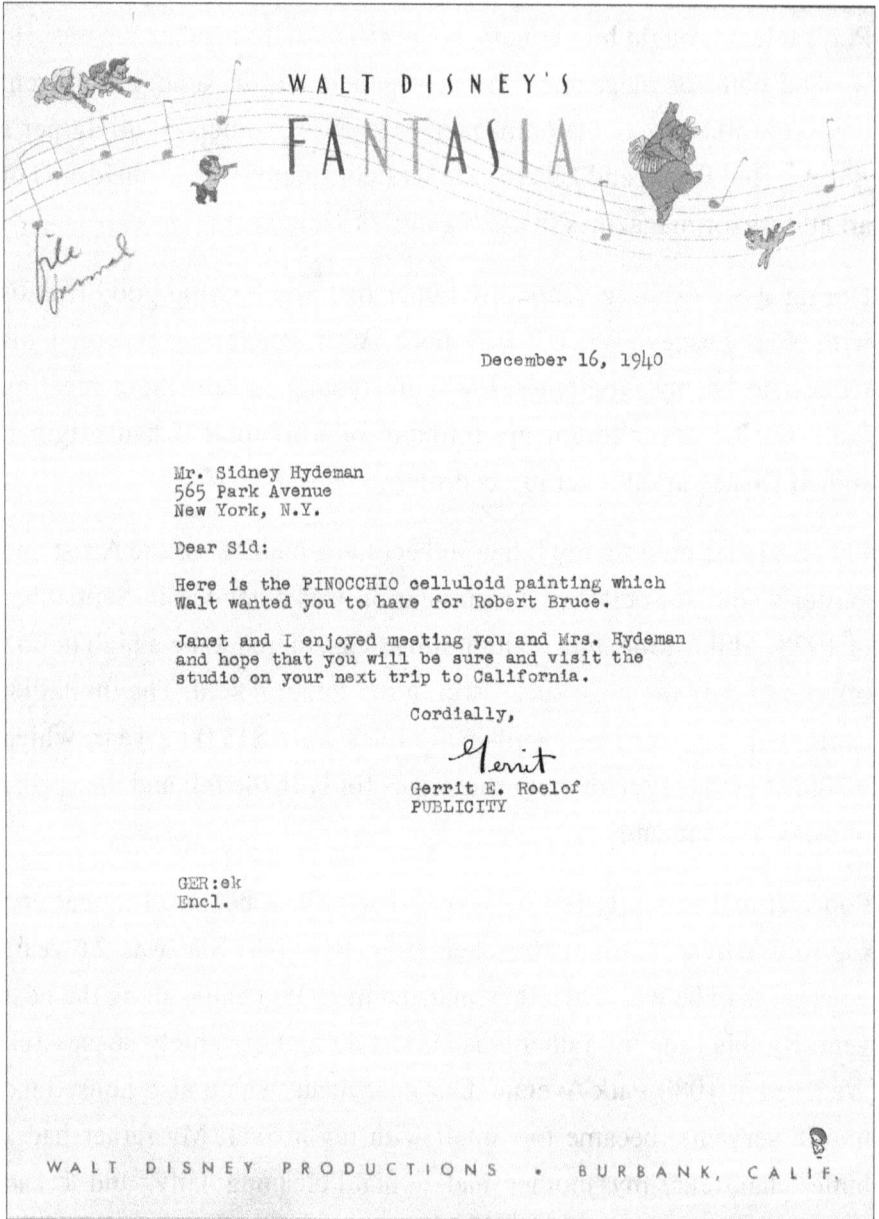

WALT DISNEY'S

FANTASIA

December 16, 1940

Mr. Sidney Hydeman
565 Park Avenue
New York, N.Y.

Dear Sid:

Here is the PINOCCHIO celluloid painting which
Walt wanted you to have for Robert Bruce.

Janet and I enjoyed meeting you and Mrs. Hydeman
and hope that you will be sure and visit the
studio on your next trip to California.

Cordially,

Gerrit E. Roelof
PUBLICITY

GER:ek
Encl.

WALT DISNEY PRODUCTIONS • BURBANK, CALIF.

The Only Ruminant I have of my Godfather Walt Disney
that survived the flood.

Artists and Writers Golf Association

Sept. 7, 1928.

Mr. Syd Hydeman,
15 West 67th. St.,
New York City

Dear Sir:-

Your name has been proposed for membership in the Artists and Writers Golf Association. The dues are $15.00 per year, and this sum includes all charges, for our Spring and Fall tournaments - dinner, prizes, green fees, etc.

Upon receipt of your check for $15.00, a membership card, entitling you to all privileges of the association, will be sent you.

Cordially yours,

Clare Briggs

CB/G   SECRETARY

My Father's Invitation to join
The Artists and Writers Golf Association.

to ours in 565 Park Avenue, also now a co-op with magnificent views, sells in the $10,000,000.00 range today. You can easily google either address to see photos of these historic buildings, along with floor plans and sales history.

I was born on October 10th, 1936. My parents, because of my father's influence, received a letter from the White House dated October 23rd, 1936 signed by Missy LeHand, the private secretary to President Franklin D. Roosevelt. Missy was thought by many to also be Roosevelt's mistress. The letter indicated that the president wanted to extend his hearty congratulations upon my birth, and wished me a "happy, active and useful life."

Since we lived in the city, and since he had a new son, Pop thought we should also have a place outside the city where we could spend time in the country enjoying the great outdoors and recreational opportunities.

A man-made lake called Candlewood Lake had been completed in 1928. Located about sixty five miles from Manhattan, near Danbury, Connecticut, it had a lot of available shoreline. It was also very undeveloped. My father bought 16 acres of mostly lake front property, and being very good with his hands, built a beautiful lake front cabin which he named Camp Hyde Away.

The plan was that my mother and I would stay there during the summer, and my father would come up for the weekends. That idea didn't fly for very long. The lake was still in the boonies, and my mother found it to be dark and scary. Before the end of the first summer, my father sold the cabin and the 16 acres for $6,000.00.

In November of 1941 my father sent a Western Union telegram to a real estate agent in Larchmont, New York with an offer to buy a home on Rye Road in Rye, New York. The neighborhood was fabulous, and

THE WHITE HOUSE
WASHINGTON

October 23, 1936

My dear Mr. and Mrs. Hydeman:

      The President has asked me to extend

to you his hearty congratulations upon the birth

of your little boy. He hopes that your son will

have a happy, active and useful life.

      Very sincerely yours,

M. a. Le Hand

M. A. LeHand
PRIVATE SECRETARY

Mr. and Mrs. Sid L. Hydeman,
1088 Park Avenue,
New York, N. Y.

THE WHITE HOUSE
OFFICIAL BUSINESS

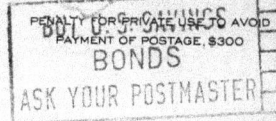

WASHINGTON D.C.
OCT 23
12-PM
1936

PENALTY FOR PRIVATE USE TO AVOID
PAYMENT OF POSTAGE, $300
BONDS
ASK YOUR POSTMASTER

Mr. and Mrs. Sid L. Hydeman,
1088 Park Avenue,
New York, N. Y.

*Letter from The White House congratulating my parents
at the time of my birth.*

even had its own private, sandy beach on Long Island Sound. His offer was for $13,500.00. The offer was countered at $13,750.00, and the deal was made. If my father had been unwilling to increase his offer by $250.00, he wouldn't have gotten the house.

My Father's original offer to purchase our home in Rye, New York

When I was eight, my parents sent me to summer camp in Maine. I went to Camp Menatoma for five summers, and I loved every minute of it. I was and am a sports nut. Each summer the campers would travel from Grand Central Station in New York City to Augusta, Maine, and at the end of camp, back to Grand Central, in sleeping cars. The camp lasted eight weeks and included deep sea fishing trips to Bar Harbor, Maine, as well as inter camp sporting competitions and mountain climbing trips to such places as Mount Washington in New Hampshire. The total cost for the summer, each year, was $400.00. Although Manatoma no longer exists, an eight-week session at a summer camp in Maine now costs over $9,000.00.

My father was a workaholic and hadn't taken a vacation for years. In 1950 he decided to make up for all that time by taking my mother, my sister and me on a four and a half month vacation to Europe. We went over and came back, first class, on the famed SS America, which at that time was the flagship of the United States Line. We visited four countries, France, England, Switzerland and Italy. We stayed in the best hotels and ate every meal in the best restaurants in every city we visited. We only traveled between destinations in the most luxurious way available, although back then, never by air.

I was only thirteen, but my father bought himself and me Rolex watches in Geneva, Switzerland. Mine was stainless steel with a stainless steel bracelet. It did not show the date. His was stainless steel and gold with a stainless steel and gold bracelet and it showed the date. Mine cost $72.00, and his cost $135.00. He bought my sister a comparable watch, and my mother was given expensive jewelry. In addition, being an artist, my father designed a family crest, and had a gold ring made to order showing the crest.

Because my sister was only ten and I was only thirteen, my parents knew we would not like to travel relentlessly. For this reason, we stayed on the Isle of Capri for three weeks, and on Lake Como at the Villa D'Este for six weeks. At that time, and to the present, the Villa D'Este is considered to be one of the finest resort hotels in the world.

This trip, in every way, was incredible. The turnkey cost of these four and a half months was $15,000.00. Immediately upon returning home, I was sent to an elite prep school. I went there for five years. The cost was $2,000.00 a year. Subsequent to that, I went to an elite college. That cost was $1,900.00 a year.

When I graduated from college in 1959, Pop sold the house and he and my mother moved into an apartment which was also in Rye. The man he sold it to was Allan Sherman who had just written a big best-selling song entitled "Hello Muddah, Hello Faddah." The selling price of the house was $60,000.00, and my father proclaimed that the house would never be worth a dime more.

Based on what I have told you about my father's success, and the luxurious life he provided his family, you will no doubt be shocked to learn that Pop never made more than $18,000.00 in any single year.

PERSPECTIVE

In 1930, my father was 35 years old. Gold was $21.00 an ounce. Back then his $18,000.00 earnings could buy over 857 ounces of gold. Using $1,200.00 an ounce as today's gold value, which is probably too low, 857 ounces of gold would be worth $1,028,400.00. Using gold as the common denominator, my father's $18,000.00 a year salary was equal in buying power to $1,028,400.00 today.

Additionally, the top Federal income tax rate on regular income in 1930 was 25% so his buying power after taxes was also better than it is today. The $15.00 annual dues for the Artist and Writer's Golf Association, with gold at $21.00 an ounce in 1928, was roughly equivalent to three quarters of an ounce of gold. Today that much gold would be worth about $900.00 which could easily pay for two greens fees, two dinners, with enough money left over to buy some prizes for two tournaments.

My father's rent on Park Avenue in New York City at $300.00 a month was cheap by today's standard, but it was not cheap back then. By this time, gold was valued at $30.00 an ounce, so my father was paying the equivalent of ten ounces of gold a month. Using the $1,200.00 an ounce formula, today that rent would be $12,000.00 a month or $144,000.00 a year.

The apartments my father was renting for $300.00 a month are in buildings that have since been co-opted. Our apartment at 565 Park Avenue was approximately 4,500 square feet. A search on the internet shows that the average selling price for the last seventeen sales in that building has been at $987.00 a square foot, making our apartment worth about $4,441,500.00. This increase in value is astonishing!

When my father bought our home in Rye, New York, gold was still in the $30.00 an ounce range. The counter offer of $250.00 was equal to about eight ounces of gold which today is worth almost $10,000.00. That counter, back then, of $250.00 was not insignificant money.

- When I went to camp, gold was $30.00 an ounce, the $400.00 cost was equal to 13.333 ounces. Using $1,200.00 an ounce for gold, that cost today would equate to $16,000.00.

- If the acreage on Candlewood Lake, which my father sold for $6,000.00, was still available today, it would be worth many millions of dollars!

- The Rolex watches in 1950 were much cheaper than they are today, but even back then, they were considered to be very expensive. The price of $72.00 was almost equal to two and a half ounces of gold which today would be $3,000.00. My father's watch at $135.00 was worth four and a half ounces of gold or $5,400.00 in today's money.

- Our $15,000.00 trip to Europe using today's gold value would have cost $600,000.00, but I really think it would have been quite a bit more than that.

- The suite we had at the Villa D'Este for six weeks is now $5,000.00 a night. That alone equals $210,000.00 for forty two days with no food included. Today, only multi-millionaires could afford that trip. Back then, my father afforded it on an income of only $18,000.00 a year.

- The boarding school I attended for $2,000.00 a year now charges $54,570.00 a year.

- My college has increased from $1,900.00 a year to $62,800.00.

- The house my father thought would never be worth more than $60,000.00 is shown on the internet to have a value of $1,778,900.00, on the low side. That is almost thirty times what he sold it for in 1959, and almost one hundred and thirty times what he paid for it in 1941!

During my father's lifetime, there was no such thing as a credit card, and obviously, there was no such thing as credit card debt. Almost everything he bought was paid for with cash. Our trip to Europe was paid in cash in the form of American Express Traveler's Cheques, which were the common form of currency for foreign travel in those days. You bought them at the bank, and carried them instead of cash while traveling because they could be replaced if stolen.

The only money my father ever borrowed was for the mortgage on his existing home. Notice on the Western Union offer he made, he offers $3,000.00 in cash, which means that he was putting down more than 20% of the purchase price. His mortgage would have only been for $10,750.00! Today, that house is worth almost $2,000,000.00. What a deal!!

Pop's Later Years

When my parents moved into the apartment in Rye, they had many things that wouldn't fit in the apartment. They stored those things in their storage unit in the basement of the apartment house. My father, being in the business, and being good friends with some of the world's greatest artists, had some extremely valuable art. This included all my Disney art, but even more importantly, two Norman Rockwell originals. Unfortunately, the basement flooded, and everything, except things in the top drawer of a file cabinet were ruined. The only Disney related item to survive the flood was the letter shown in the exhibit, which had been filed in that cabinet. Those Rockwells alone, would be worth millions today.

By this time, 1959, my father was 64, retired and trying to be frugal, and insurance on the artwork would have been extremely expensive. None of the art was insured and it was a total loss.

This chapter does not have a happy ending. My father lived to be 86, but his money didn't last nearly as long as he did. When he retired, he had what he expected to be more than enough money to support my mother and himself throughout their lifetimes.

Inflation and longevity had other ideas. Our father died insolvent and left my sister and me financially responsible for our mother's well being.

A CHARMED LIFE ENDS

My father's generation had a totally different perspective on life and longevity than we have today. My grandfather died at the age of 46. Pop thought he would be lucky to reach the age of 60 and planned his finances accordingly. He did not believe in life insurance. From his perspective, his much younger wife would only be 39, still attractive, and would remarry a rich man and live happily ever after.

Pop was an artist, not a businessman. He lived from day to day with no long range plan, and he had no supplemental sources of income except interest on his savings account. He retired with the confidence that he had enough money to live the rest of his life comfortably.

My father was shocked at how expensive things had become over the course of his life. When we look back, we think how inexpensive things were back then. Pop did not have the benefit of over a hundred years of practical history, which this book portrays, in order to be able to see the trends of where he was financially when he retired, versus where he would be financially when he died.

This book is all about those trends, which I call the Big Four. My mother and father were victims who suffered because of trends that they never had a chance to recognize. Today's world has become much more complicated, and there are now even more trends and much more powerful trends than existed during their lifetimes.

Please take the lesson in this chapter seriously. Being insolvent is no way to spend your old age, and your old age may be a lot longer than you expect. As you will see in later chapters, Social Security may or may not be available to you. Social Security, if available, is great supplemental income, but believe me, it is not a standalone comfortable living wage.

Unlike my father, you have the ability to recognize and understand the Big Four. You need to pay attention to this shot across the bow. To avoid the disaster of poverty in your later years, you must take charge of your financial future. You must also recognize and believe that you are the only person you can count on to do so.

The consequences of not steering your financial ship yourself are devastating. My father's story should be considered your shot across the bow. If you're not convinced, continue with me on my trip through the Hydeman family history and read my own story next.

CHAPTER 2

BOB GOES TO WORK

I graduated from college in 1959 with a Bachelor of Arts Degree. My father had made it clear that he would pay for four years of college, not a minute more, and after that I was strictly on my own.

During my senior year, I was perplexed about what I wanted to do or be professionally. I knew a number of things I didn't want to do or couldn't have done. So I worked backward through the process of elimination, and decided that my best option was to work for a big company, climb the corporate ladder, become Chairman of the Board, be retired at 65, have a dinner given in my honor at which I would be awarded a gold watch, and then I would be sent on my merry way. I would then move to an elaborate beach house in Florida, travel extensively, and wear out some golf courses.

It seemed like a good plan, and in my youthful exuberance, I was confident in my ability to achieve those goals. No sweat!

ACCORDING TO PLAN

I was interviewed on campus by several Forbes 100 companies, and I was fortunate enough to have several offers. The best offer, I thought, came from the Continental Can Company. Continental Can offered me $450.00 a month with the promise of a $50.00 a month raise after six months. I couldn't believe my good fortune, and several of my college professors expressed jealousy at my starting salary.

Even much more impressive than my salary were the fringe benefits.

- CCC had a major medical plan that covered just about every medical contingency for the employee and his family.

- They had a stock plan that entitled each employee to one share of stock for every $500.00 of earnings. Since my annual salary was at the rate of $6,000.00, at the end of the first year, I was awarded 12 shares of stock. At that time, the stock had a value of about $50.00 a share, so I was given a benefit worth about $600.00.

- The company offered life insurance and disability policies based on income.

- They had profit sharing, and very importantly, they had a great retirement plan that started at age 65.

- All the company employees were automatically retired on their sixty fifth birthday.

Continental Can emphasized that they were "taking care of their own" by providing not only a living wage, but also "security" for life. There was no doubt in my mind that my career would start and end with the Continental Can Company.

At the time of my hiring, Continental Can was the 34th largest company in America. It was the largest packaging company in the world. It not only had a can division, but also a corrugated box division, a folding carton division, a flexible packaging division and a paper plate and paper cup division.

I was hired as an executive sales trainee in the folding carton division. The company explained that it would spend $50,000.00, and at least six months preparing me to become a knowledgeable professional folding carton sales person.

Disappointingly, my career with
Continental Can Company
lasted only six years.

During that time I was in and out of the Army twice. The first tour was for six months and I had a rank of Recruit E1, which paid $72.00 a month.

I was recalled for a second tour during the Berlin Crisis for approximately eight months. By this time I had been promoted twice to the rank of PFC, E-3, which increased my salary to $92.00 a month.

After my second tour in the Army, I returned to Continental Can in 1961 to find a very different business environment. I realized that my original thought of being with one company forever needed to be amended. I was devastated at the thought of changing jobs, but Continental Can was experiencing serious financial problems, and had instituted an austerity plan that froze salaries and promotions. Shortly after my second tour in the army, I had married, and sixteen months later, we had our first child. That same year, we bought our first house, and Continental Can was only paying me an embarrassing $6,600.00 a year. My wife had quit her job as a second grade school teacher to take care of our son. She had been making more than I had been making. Her salary had been $7,200.00 a year.

Fortunately, the house we bought was very affordable. It was in my home town of Rye, New York, and it had been built as a summer cottage in 1919. It was two blocks from a city beach on Long Island Sound. The house had already benefited from a facelift, and it was a great starting home. It had three very small bedrooms, only one bathroom, a big living room with a beautiful stone fireplace, a kitchen, a dining room and a screened in porch. It sat on an eighth of an acre, and the house was only about 1,200 square feet.

We purchased the home for $20,300.00. My mother was the real estate agent, and she gave us her commission as part of our down payment. The mortgage on the house was only $104.25 a month. At the time we bought the house, banks were paying 5% interest on savings accounts, and $100,000.00 certificates of deposit were paying 6%. It made sense, at this time, to save money as part of an investment strategy.

I started my job search by going to a "headhunter". I felt guilty, as I was still working at Continental Can. I was somewhat embarrassed, and the sense that I was sneaking around just added to my feelings of failure. However, he was excited about what he could do for me and even had a client who was looking for someone with exactly my background and training.

The company he introduced me to was a brand new division of Time, Inc. Time had just acquired a major paper company called East Texas Pulp and Paper (Eastex) which had a folding carton division, Eastex Packaging, that needed a second salesman in New York City. The interview went well, and I got the job. The salary was, in my opinion at the time, a "whopping $10,000.00." The offer included all the fringe benefits I had depended on at Continental Can.

But this company was very different than a company on austerity. They were aggressive and supportive and allowed the field sales force to really go after the business. My first year with the company was so successful that they increased my salary by $100.00 a month three different times. It was now 1966, I was making $13,600.00 a year, and I felt very confident about the future.

The second year was a total turn around. The company was experiencing growth pains, and it couldn't maintain its product quality. The division lost customers and money.

Having launched my career in 1959, I now found myself in 1967. Back then, being with a big company implied job security and an overall feeling of security. Employees believed their employer was like a big brother who would protect them in every way possible, and this would continue for a very long time. Continental Can did not survive. Neither did Eastex.

I realized that it was time for me change direction, and find something to sell other than paper boxes.

CHAPTER 3

TIME TO RETHINK MY PLAN

After two bad experiences in the packaging business, I decided to change my luck by changing industries. I was amazed by how difficult this turned out to be, but I did manage to land on my feet as a marketing manager with the United States Leasing Corporation.

At the time, U.S. Leasing was listed on the American Stock Exchange, and it was the largest third party general equipment lessor in the country. U.S. Leasing was a great employer back in those days. They were the preferred national leasing company for the three largest business machine manufacturers in the world.

It was my job to convince their salespeople to offer their equipment to their customers on a U.S. lease rather than on an outright purchase. The concept was very simple and beneficial to all.

- U.S. Leasing benefited by profiting on the signed three, five or eight year lease.

- The equipment salesman got his purchase order from the leasing company instead of directly from the customer,

- The customer got the equipment for a low monthly payment which was a tax deductible business expense.

This should have been a fabulous business opportunity. I called on branch offices all over New York City that had equipment salesmen who had been told by their management that my leasing company was the company of choice. However, I ran into a big snag.

I worked diligently with the salesmen and their sales managers only to find out that my competition was paying 2% kickbacks to the salesman who brought leases to them. When a salesman got a $20,000.00 signed lease for the leasing company, he not only earned his sales commission from his company, but he also got a $400.00 kickback from the leasing company. The salesmen were very happy with the extra money, which, for some, became a lot of money, and the sales managers turned a blind eye because their people had an added incentive to make more deals. I couldn't overcome the kickback challenge, and after about a year, for the first and only time in my life, I was fired!

The only place I knew to go was to the "headhunter" who had gotten me the job with Eastex Packaging. I told him that I wanted to change professions because of the kickback situation. He told me to keep an open mind because my experience and training with U.S. Leasing was very valuable.

The headhunter got me an interview with Magnavox for the position of National Marketing Manager for a new product called a "Telecopier." The Telecopier was the very early version of a machine that could send a paper copy of a document across the country in four minutes. This, of course, became what we know today as a fax machine. Magnavox later sold the rights to the Telecopier to Xerox, and the rest is history.

Magnavox made me an offer of $16,000.00 a year in salary, with all the fringe benefits. My wife and I were thrilled with Magnavox, a major company listed on the New York Stock Exchange. We loved the National Marketing Manager title, and we loved the compensation package.

We told the headhunter that we were ready to accept the deal. The headhunter told me that he wanted me to take one more interview before I took the job. Without speaking to me, he had spoken to the sales manager at the rival leasing company that had been paying the kickbacks that got me fired. The man wanted to meet with me. I told the headhunter in no uncertain terms that I had no interest in meeting with him.

The headhunter came back and said the man wanted to buy me a shrimp cocktail and the best steak in town at Peter Luger's, and he wanted to talk. It was an offer I couldn't refuse.

We had a great lunch, and a great discussion. I told him I didn't like the kickback business, and he said that he was going to assign me to the Honeywell computer account, and there were no kickbacks in the major computer market.

He offered me a salary of $15,000.00 a year with 2% commissions on everything I sold. The package included all the fringe benefits, a very generous expense account, and a brand new top of the line Buick Roadmaster company car. I accepted the offer before we had dessert.

The name of the company was Leasco Data Processing Equipment Corporation. Like Magnavox, it was a New York Stock Exchange Company. In fact, at that time, Leasco had reached a billion dollars in sales faster than any company in New York Stock Exchange history.

Like U.S. Leasing, Leasco was a third party equipment lessor that did big volumes of business with office equipment vendors. However, Leasco created a huge new market by leasing mainframe computers at a lease rate well below the manufacturer's lease rate. If someone wanted to lease an IBM computer, Leasco's monthly payment for that computer was significantly less than IBM's.

This was at the time when major corporations were making huge investments in their computer equipment, and Leasco, much to the consternation of IBM, and their competitors, was doing much of the leasing business. The company's reputation and stock soared. It was the darling of Wall Street.

One of the first things I did after joining Leasco was to go to a convention in Atlantic City at which Honeywell was exhibiting. By fate, I met Al Fisher who had been in purchasing with the American Can company which was Continental Can's closest rival. Our can company backgrounds gave us something in common, and we decided to have lunch together.

Al was about twenty years older than I was, and he had just accepted the job of Director of Purchasing at the Roosevelt Hospital in New York City. While at lunch, I asked him if the hospital had ever leased any of its equipment. His answer was "no," and he wondered why they would since they "had all the money in the world." I explained the benefits of leasing, and Al became very intrigued. He asked me if I would make a presentation to the hospital's Board of Directors. I jumped at the opportunity!

After I made my presentation to the Roosevelt Hospital board, the chairman asked me if we could create a master lease to which we could add addendums for each piece of new equipment that the hospital wanted to acquire. When I told him that we could do that, he instructed Al Fischer to contract for every piece of capital equipment that the hospital needed in the future using my master lease. This was the beginning of the third party hospital equipment leasing business.

After we had our program up and running, I asked Al if he would introduce me to some of his contemporaries in other major hospitals in New York City. He and I had become good friends, and he was more than happy to help me. I was fortunate enough to make similar arrangements with giant hospitals including the New York Hospital, Beth Israel, Brooklyn Eye and Ear and a number of lesser known hospitals. I gave up the Honeywell computer account to concentrate on my hospital business which, with 2% commissions, was making me a lot of money every month.

It is said that all good things must come to an end. Leasco proved that by coming to a very abrupt end. The company had been founded by a 22 year old graduate of the Wharton Business School by the name of Saul Steinberg. Saul was the genius who created the third party computer leasing business. He realized that a company like Leasco needed a strong financial statement with a heavy emphasis on cash. Creatively, he arranged to acquire the Reliance Insurance Company which had much more cash than Leasco, and Saul was able to leverage this with the banks to grow his leasing business. Everything was going so well, that Saul decided to acquire the Chemical Bank in New York City.

He announced his intention prematurely, and the banking establishment took strong and immediate action to quell the acquisition. The banks' actions made the cost of money to Leasco so high that Leasco could no longer compete in any aspect of the leasing business. Leasco immediately went from number one to number none. Leasco, including me, was completely out of business. Saul, until his recent death, remained the CEO of the very successful Reliance Insurance Company.

Knowing that I wanted to stay in the hospital equipment leasing business, I went to my friend Al Fisher and asked him who he would be leasing from if he wasn't doing business with me. Al indicated that there was a start-up company that had a unique approach to leasing hospital equipment. To begin with, unlike Leasco, the company only leased hospital equipment.

The company's name was Technical Equipment Leasing Corporation. Telco was the first "specialty hospital equipment leasing company." Because most of the company employees had medical equipment sales experience, they could offer trade-ins to the hospital when the hospital wanted to upgrade their equipment. The company had a used equipment division called Labex that refurbished the equipment that the leasing company had taken as a trade–in, and, then Labex could resell it to secondary hospitals at a substantial profit.

The ability to make a profit with used equipment gave Telco a huge competitive advantage. Because they knew the future value of the equipment they were leasing, they could offer a much higher residual value to the new equipment they were leasing, and their lease rates were way below the market.

Telco was headquartered in Chicago, and I called the founder of the company, Marty Zimmerman, and told him that Al Fisher suggested that I call him. Marty indicated that he would be on the next plane to New York, and we agreed where to meet.

In the meeting Marty explained that the company was in its infancy. They had a President of the Labex Division, and they had regional leasing managers in New York, Chicago, and Los Angeles. The position he needed to fill was for a regional manager somewhere in the south. Marty's offer to me was to be the number two guy in New York, or to be the number one guy in whichever major city I choose in the South. Marty agreed, if I took the job in the south, he would continue to compensate me for future business done in the hospital accounts I had originated in New York.

The compensation package was the same for both jobs. A salary of $18,000.00, a 2% commission on my personal sales, all the fringe benefits, a very generous expense account, a company car and two additional perks that I had never previously been offered.

Because it was a privately owned start-up company, Marty could offer his employees stock options that could become very valuable when the company went public. Going public was definitely Marty's intention.

Additionally, the southern region included twelve states, and it would become my responsibility to build a sales force to cover that territory. I would earn overrides on the sales of the people I hired. This means I would make additional compensation as they produced business.

My wife and I discussed our options. We decided that the risk of moving was worth taking because this would be my first opportunity to manage a huge territory with the potential for big commissions and overrides on the people I hired and managed, and because the stock could make us rich.

It was 1969. This would be my fifth job. Three of them, Continental Can, Eastex Packaging and Leasco had been New York Stock companies. One of them had already failed, and the other two were failing. In the fourth, U.S. Leasing, an American Stock Exchange company I had failed. But, as best I can tell, U.S. Leasing is now defunct. I had always been with established, major stock exchange companies that I had wrongly thought offered long term security. I was about to move to a part of the country where I knew no one, to work with a company no one had ever heard of.

I was definitely out of my comfort zone, but I was excited about the potential of the opportunity.

CHAPTER 4

TEXAS, HERE WE COME

My wife, our two children and I moved to Dallas, Texas in 1969. We had sold our house in Rye for a very good profit, and we were qualified to pay as much as $55,000.00 for a new home. We were shocked and delighted to find that a $55,000.00 house in Dallas would have cost well over $100,000.00 in our old home town. We bought our dream home for exactly what we qualified for.

I went to work looking for office space and I hired a secretary. Even though I was brand new in the south, and talked like a 'damn Yankee', my business exploded. Because of the way Telco treated the residual values of the equipment we were leasing, and because of our ability to take trade-ins, the lease payments we were able to quote were thirty percent and more beneath our competition. Often, when we bid on a lease, the hospital administrator would call to make sure we hadn't made a mistake. We had to explain why our payments were so low, and when we did, we had a new hospital customer.

It got to the point that our repeat customers called in to add pieces of equipment, and new customers signed up over the phone based on our reputation, and referrals in the industry. We had the best product in the world. Our product was a financial service providing capital for equipment leasing, and we were selling it at a price hospitals couldn't refuse.

During this time, I had hired twelve salesmen in my region, and they were all doing extremely well. The company had expanded nationally to fifty five salesmen. Telco's corporate sales exceeded, $100,000,000.00, and the Board of Directors voted to take the company public on the NASDAQ Exchange.

Over the course of time, I had earned stock options, and I borrowed money to buy as much additional stock as I could. All this stock fell under Rule 144, which meant that it had a two year restriction on it before I could sell it. The initial offering of the stock was explosive. The first tick over the counter was for forty nine dollars a share.

On paper, I had an excellent net worth, but it was money I couldn't access for at least two years, and in the meanwhile, I had the risk of being heavily in debt.

Telco had made a tragic mistake.

They were borrowing short and lending long. All their short term loans, which were for a year or less, were tied to the prime rate. Their leases were written for a fixed rate for up to eight years. Telco hedged their bet by factoring their cost of money based on a prime rate of 10%. Telco thought the prime rate would never go that high, and they felt very secure that they were well protected from interest rate hikes.

Unfortunately, as history shows, the prime rate hit record highs, and every lease Telco had written was cash flow negative. My stock went from $49.00 a share to being worthless. My debt continued to grow dramatically because of the extremely high interest rates.

Debt is a two edged sword. From a positive standpoint, debt provides great leverage to take advantage of opportunities that work out well. From a negative standpoint, it can become a heavy burden if the opportunity fails. It's the classic challenge and balance of risk versus reward.

Banks are in the business of making loans to individuals and business entities of every description. These loans are called "liabilities" on a balance sheet. The challenge is to convert those loan liabilities into assets and profits on the asset and net worth side of the balance sheet.

My experiences in the leasing business had been a roller coaster ride.

I had gone from having the highest net worth and the best cash flow I had ever had to the lowest net worth and no cash flow, and I had done it all in near record time. I was now deeply in debt, and out of work.

By now it was 1973, and I was convinced that I had run the course in the leasing business and it was time, yet again, to change industries.

Chapter 5

NO BUSINESS IS BULLET PROOF

Up to this point, job security and the security of having great corporate benefits had always been extremely important considerations for me when choosing my employer. While things were going well with Telco, I had invested in some raw land deals with a man who had just graduated from college, and who was doing extremely well. The syndication of raw land, and the flipping of those syndications, was booming in Texas, and it seemed as if that might be something that I could be interested in doing professionally.

Real estate held a lot of interest for me because I had seen what had happened with my father's real estate holdings, as well as what had happened with my first home. I had never seen a real estate deal that hadn't done well.

Going into the real estate business was going to require a lot of thought.

- To begin with, I was broke and deeply in debt.

- Real estate sales required a state license which required taking courses and passing tests.

- Being a real estate agent was entrepreneurial. There was no salary.

- The compensation was commissions only, and there were no corporate benefits.

There were some aspects to the real estate business that were very appealing to me. For one thing, I had been traveling extensively with Telco. I had a twelve state territory in the south, and a corporate home office in Chicago. I was always going somewhere. I had a wife and two young kids, and I wanted to stay home with them. Real estate, as I envisioned it, required much less travel.

Additionally, real estate was a product that was not only good to sell from a commission standpoint, but as an investment it could also be very good to own. On top of that, real estate is a business in which a successful agent can become an entrepreneur and, at the right time, open his own agency.

Need and greed were big components of my decision. I needed to get out of debt, and the opportunity to make really big commissions excited me. It looked to me that the really big money was in commercial rather than residential real estate. Commercial real estate deals were often much bigger, and therefore more lucrative, than residential, although I have since seen that residential real estate can also be a great way to make money.

The man who had been selling me interests in raw land syndications had, with three partners, just formed his own company, and they agreed to make me their first employee. It was both very exciting, but also very intense.

For the first time in my business experience, I had no support system. There was no salary. There were no fringe benefits. If I didn't perform and sell something, my family would go hungry and we could lose everything. That's what is known as motivation!

I survived my first year in the business by the skin of my teeth. As hot as the raw land syndication business had been, the cycle ended, and raw land became an ice cold commodity. The four partners were about to go in different directions and I needed to consolidate and fight my way out of the hole I had dug for myself. By this time, I had acquired my broker's license, so I could be in business for myself.

In order to minimize my overhead, I moved my office into the house and aggressively pursued the sales of income producing properties. Working out of the house and being a broker proved to be smart moves. A sales agent has to share his commissions with his broker. As a broker, I got to keep all the commissions I earned without having to share with anyone, and because my overhead in the house was low, I was able to pay off my debt and generate positive cash flow.

Things started to really heat up. I teamed up with several developers who were building and leasing retail shopping centers and office buildings, and I had the privilege of selling those properties. Additionally, I had a developer who developed almost two hundred condominiums on South Padre Island, and I had the privilege of selling almost all of them to investors and second home buyers. Things were going so well that I bought a three bedroom penthouse unit on the top floor of the last project.

Then things just went crazy! The savings and loans in Texas, and all the banks had more money than they knew what to do with, and they needed places to invest it. If a developer had a property and a plan, lenders came out of the woodwork to fight to make that loan. Everyone around me was making a fortune, so I jumped on the band wagon and became a partner in a number of projects. As a partner, you sign loan agreements with personal liability. I had no compunctions about signing loan agreements. Texas was growing like a weed, and Dallas was leading the way. The banks and the S&Ls were begging us to take their money.

My business had grown to the point that I had moved out of the house, taken expensive office space, bought expensive office furniture and computers, hired ten commissioned sales and leasing people and had three salaried employees. My monthly overhead had grown from practically nothing to $30,000.00 a month. As the exclusive leasing broker for several developers, I found myself on a very hot seat. My agents and I were having a terrible time finding tenants for the properties we represented. I was not only the leasing broker, but also a partner with personal liability in these empty properties.

I got a call from my primary bank in downtown Dallas with whom I had a sizeable loan on a line of credit. They invited me to lunch in their executive dining room. At the luncheon, they explained that they were thrilled to have me as a customer, and they wanted to increase my line of credit. I thanked them for the lunch, but I told them that I was comfortable with my existing line, and I didn't envision needing more credit.

Less than two months later I got a call from the same bank. This time it was from an elderly gentleman who explained that he was an eighty year old retired "work out specialist" whom the bank had rehired to handle problem loans for the bank. I told him that all my loans were current, and I had no problem loans. His explanation was that the bank had determined that the real estate market was in disarray, and the bank was calling all its real estate related loans.

This was the beginning of what became known as the S&L crisis in Texas, but it was very much more than that. It became a local depression in both the banking and the real estate businesses in the state. Every S&L went broke and the FSLIC closed and locked their doors. A number of S&L officers and directors went to jail.

The largest banks in the state were financially destroyed. My bank, Interfirst Bank, was the largest bank in the state. They merged with Republic Bank, the second largest in the state, in an effort to survive. The merged banks became First Republic Bank, and within a year they became, at that time, the largest bank failure in U.S. history.

MBank, the third largest bank in the state also failed. In fact, all but one sizeable bank in the state failed, and they were bailed out by healthy, major, out of state banks. First Republic was acquired by the Bank of America, and MBank was acquired by Nationsbank.

Texas, one of the richest states in the union, had virtually no home based major banks. The over building in the largest real estate markets in Texas had destroyed the banks, and real estate values plummeted. Real estate owners, developers and investors filed for bankruptcy in droves. The federal government came in with an agency called the "Resolution Trust Corporation" in order to restore sanity and value to all the distressed properties in the state.

I learned in the hardest way possible, by being in the middle of it, that nothing is invulnerable. Not even the banking system or the real estate markets in one of the strongest economies in the world.

CHAPTER 6

COLD AND CRUEL

It has been said that the world is a cold, cruel place. It really is. Just watch.

With everything falling apart around me, I refused to declare bankruptcy. I was either honorable or stupid, or just stupidly honorable.

I traded everything I owned to the banks in lieu of all my debt. This included all my commercial real estate holdings, my penthouse condominium on South Padre Island, a lake house in Connecticut, and even my homestead. I had no money, no credit, no job and no home. I was extremely lucky to still have a family. My wife went back to work in the executive offices of Saks Fifth Avenue. We found a low cost rental apartment that accepted us, and I worked out of the apartment in an effort to make deals in the distressed real estate market.

When there are no real estate lenders, there are very few real estate buyers, but there were some "bottom fisherman" paying cash for properties priced at pennies on the dollar. I had a huge challenge. I needed to buy a nice home for my family without any money or any credit, or any employer. I needed a lender who would make me a loan that would cover all my closing costs and 100% of the purchase price of the house. This seemed less possible than finding a needle in a big hay stack!

Believe it or not, I found the perfect home in the perfect neighborhood, and it was owned by the perfect seller. The house had been foreclosed on by MBank. It had been owned by a wealthy developer who had let it go back to the lender.

There were thousands of foreclosures in the Dallas-Fort Worth Metroplex, and even at distressed prices, with no lenders, there were very few buyers. I told the real estate agent, who was a real pro, exactly what challenges I was facing. He explained that MBank really needed to divest itself of this house, and the bankers in the real estate department of the bank all knew that they were about to lose their jobs, and that MBank was about to be acquired.

My agent gave me a very low price at which he believed he could deliver the house and all the necessary financing, even with my challenges. I am convinced it was the only house anywhere that I could have been able to purchase. That was twenty eight years ago, and my wife and I still live in that house, and we still love it.

In this cold cruel world, it helps to be lucky. In this instance I was very lucky. Some people say they would rather be lucky than good. Given a preference, I'd rather be both, good and lucky! They are very important qualities in this cold cruel world.

But here is another very important rule. Don't be afraid to ask for favors. People like to help people they like, and if they can help someone, it makes them feel better about themselves. So it's a win, win deal.

The worst thing that can happen is they say "no," and that didn't cost you anything. If you ask for something you want, you might just get it. Give yourself a chance. If you don't ask, you have no chance, and you definitely won't get it!

CHAPTER 7

A TOUGH NEW BEGINNING

We moved into our new house on March 1st, 1989.

Locally, real estate and the banks were in a depression, and I felt a lot of stress trying to live up to our financial obligations. Our daughter was in a private college, and our mortgage payment on the new house was by far the biggest I had ever committed to. I had two other big expenses, Life Insurance and Disability Insurance, which were bones of contention between my wife and me.

My wife, who, I admit in hindsight, is almost always right, claimed that we were "insurance poor." Our monthly insurance premiums were costing us a big percentage of our income. While things were going extremely well in the real estate business, I had bought the best insurance benefits my income qualified for. I kept making the payments on those policies because I knew that my current income would not allow me nearly as much coverage as I had, and I thought it was important, for the security of the family, that I maintain the policies at the high limits. The policies were for both life insurance and disability insurance.

My wife's argument was that I never got sick and that I would probably live to be a hundred. She wanted me to cancel the policies and save the premiums. Even though when I argue with her I am usually wrong, I stuck to my guns. I explained to her that the policies were irreplaceable, and if, God forbid, something happened to me, she and the kids would be financially protected. Unfortunately, in this one instance, I turned out to be right.

After we had been in the new house for less than six months, I woke up with my head turned to the left, and I couldn't straighten it out. If I was sitting in the driver's seat of my car, I would have been looking out the left front window of the car. I couldn't even turn my head far enough to the right to see the front windshield. My wife took me to the doctor who quickly recognized my condition as a chronic neurological disorder which was irreversible and incurable.

The doctor referred me to a neurologist who reconfirmed the diagnosis and recommended some possible treatments. None of the treatments were cures, and they all had potentially serious and, some even potentially, fatal, side effects.

For once, unfortunately, I had been right about insisting on keeping our insurance intact. The disability insurance company doctor declared me "disabled for life," and my policy paid me enough money to maintain our lifestyle.

This is an extremely important message:
If you possibly can, get the biggest disability insurance policy
you can qualify for and afford.

Many people who have life insurance, discount the importance of disability insurance. During much of one's life, the chances of becoming disabled are far greater than they are of dying. Disability insurance is very expensive, and a terrible waste of money, until you need it, and then it becomes the best money you ever spent.

Hope for the best, but plan for the worst.

CHAPTER 8

"NEVER, NEVER, NEVER GIVE UP"

One of the many things Winston Churchill is famous for is having said "Never, never, never give up." He also said, "If you're going through hell, keep going," and "Success is the ability to go from failure to failure without losing your enthusiasm." When the medical prognosis is that you have a chronic, incurable condition, the patient has two choices. He can accept the prognosis, or he can look for solutions to improve his situation.

I was definitely going through hell, but I did keep going. I went to all different kinds of medical practitioners hoping for help, but it was like going from failure to failure. I couldn't afford to lose my enthusiasm about finding help, and I couldn't afford to give up. If I had given up, the people I would have abandoned would have been my family and myself.

Unthinkable!

In the real world, each person needs to make his own luck. For three years I had been a vegetable. I couldn't read or write, and I certainly couldn't drive a car. My wife took me from doctor to doctor. We investigated every conventional medical option, and every alternative medical option. By luck, a friend of mine recommended an Oriental Medical Doctor who had helped his wife.

After examining me, the doctor said he could help, but it was going to be a very long and very intense treatment. I started going to him three days a week. The treatment was originated five thousand years ago in

Korea, and this doctor was the only practitioner in the United States. His office was three miles from my house. In this case, being lucky was much better than being good.

The treatment was even more intense than I had anticipated. It was partly deep, deep muscle massage which included the doctor, and sometimes him and his associate standing on my back and legs and driving their feet into my muscles. Once in awhile, I would pass out, and when they revived me and asked me if I was okay, I'd tell them, "Go deeper!" At the end of the first year, I knew we were making progress. When I thanked the doctor for what he was doing for me, he said, "Thank yourself. Everybody else I know would have quit."

As a kid, I played a lot of sports, some at a fairly high level. I learned the adage that "Quitters never win, and winners never quit." Sports really are a microcosm of life.

My condition is not life threatening, but it certainly can destroy the quality of life. I am not fully recovered, and I never will be, but my Oriental Medical Doctor restored much of my quality of life. I can never thank him enough!

One other extremely important thing to point out is the fact that my wife never, never quit or gave up on me! Without her, I would have had no chance whatsoever. I try to thank her every day!

After almost five years of going through hell, I was ready to try to reenter the workforce.

CHAPTER 9

BACK TO WORK

When my doctor made the original diagnosis, I told him I was going to make a comeback. He was nice enough to tell me that as bad my condition was, nobody ever had ever recovered to the point of being fully functional. He went on to add that my condition had one of the highest suicide rates.

He quickly became my ex doctor. His negative comments gave me additional motivation to prove him wrong! In my ex doctor's face, I was going back to work. Whatever it took.

By 1994, I was ready to look for a job. I told the disability insurance company that I didn't need the coverage for that condition any longer. They exempted the condition from the policy going forward. Talk about being stupid! My policy, for that condition, would have paid me to age 65. I had paid for that coverage for years, and I forfeited over a million dollars' worth of the benefits to which, according to the policy, I was legally entitled! I had just set a new world's record for being brain dead!

In looking for something to do professionally, I had determined that I had been burned out of real estate and I needed a new beginning.

I investigated every opportunity that crossed my desk. I interviewed for jobs relentlessly, and I got turned down for every job relentlessly. It became apparent that I had at least three strikes against me.

- In the first place, I was considered too old. An employer could find younger, well qualified people who had lower salary requirements, more energy, and much better technology skills.

- Secondly, I was too entrepreneurial. Employers were afraid that after they trained me, I might become their competition.

- And, thirdly, my disability is highly visible, and employers considered me to be too sick and a liability on their health insurance coverage.

There is a lesson here that each reader needs to figure out for himself. Here it is:

> *What I learned trying to re-enter the workforce after five years out of it, was that I was on my own.*

My last formal job interview has now been over 22 years ago, and I haven't had a formal job since my diagnosis, nearly 30 years ago. Everything I've done since then has been through self-employment. My compensation has been commissions only. Each of us has a different background and different skill sets, and each of us needs to figure out how to best utilize that background and those skills to maximize his or her long term earnings challenges. Why? The federal government won't have the budget to fund your old age, and your company and/or personal savings probably won't either!

You have now had a quick real-life tour of 100 years worth of how jobs, benefits, income and the value of the dollar have changed and affected real people. Sid Hydeman's story began in the early part of the 20th century, and mine has now extended through the same period of the 21st century. You've seen what the dollar could buy on Pop's $18K annual salary and now contrasted it to how much more money was required for me to make a living and give my family a much less luxurious lifestyle than I enjoyed growing up.

We all use the phrase "cost of living" without necessarily digging into what that means. As we move into Part II, I want to go into detail about the Big Four - the unstoppable trends that none of us can avoid, and all of us must reckon with as we seek to keep our ship afloat for a lifetime journey.

If you haven't yet recognized that the century-long Hydeman story is YOUR shot across the bow, read on. You will.

PART II

THE BIG FOUR

Chapter 10

UNSTOPPABLE AND UNAVOIDABLE

At the heart of why my family's 100-year snippet of history should matter to you is the existence of four pervasive trends that cannot be stopped and cannot be avoided.

"The Big Four"

Devaluation of the dollar

Consider Pop's lifestyle (without credit cards) on $18K a year.

Technology

Automation comes with a human cost.

National Debt

Go look at usnationaldebtclock.org for five minutes. Sobering.

Longevity

Our lifespans are greatly increased from what they were 100 years ago.

If you have any illusion that the Big Four have not or will not have much effect on you or your children, you need to pay attention to every word, every statistic and every example in this section of the book. These are not trends that are unique to this generation, with perhaps the exception of the national debt. The difference now is that we have captured enough data AND history to draw some inescapable conclusions. Chief among your concerns should be how you will pay for a life that lasts 25% longer than it would have in another generation. Are you going to just work longer? I became disabled in my early 50s. Can you save enough to combat the continuing loss of buying power of the dollar? Good luck with that. What happens when your job is automated and you're no longer needed? Think about it. Finally, will your Social Security and Medicare benefits survive the country's national debt? There is a very real possibility that they may not. Even if they do, will it be adequate to support you in the lifestyle you'll be comfortable with?

I'd say I'm not trying to frighten you, but I'd be lying. You SHOULD be concerned about caring for future you!

This IS your warning shot.

Chapter 11

EVERYTHING WE THOUGHT WE KNEW HAS CHANGED

As a kid growing up in New York, the only cars I remember seeing until I was about 15 were all built in America.

The year was 1951. Detroit was the car capital of the world. Remember, the Second World War had only ended about five years previously, so we weren't seeing any cars imported from our former enemies, Germany and Japan.

The Big Three car manufacturers in this country were, and still are, General Motors, Ford and Chrysler, but back then there were a number of other American car companies that didn't survive. The deceased include such once-famous names as Studebaker, Packard, and American Motors, among others.

No one of my father's generation would have ever believed that any of the Big Three could possibly fail financially. The fact that two of the three did declare bankruptcy, and only survived because of government bailouts, is indicative of what is happening faster and faster in the world of business. The Big Three now compete globally with multiple, powerful companies from Japan, Sweden, Germany, England and South Korea, among others, for the world's car and truck business.

Detroit's dominance in the car business, and its economy have been destroyed, at least for now. On July 18th, 2013, Detroit became the largest American City ever to file for bankruptcy.

The car industry is just one prime example of what has happened, and what continues to happen to manufacturing jobs in America.

Another perfect example, and one that is highly visible and close to home, is television sets. When my wife and I married in 1963, all televisions were made in America. The only brands we had ever even heard of were RCA, Zenith, Motorola, Philco, Sylvania, and Dumont. Guess where all that business went. Just look at the name brand on your T.V. to find the answer.

The global economy and technology are changing very rapidly and decimating the American job market. Globally, jobs are going to Mexico and overseas because the labor markets and corporate tax rates are much lower than they are domestically. Some recent examples of job migration from this country include Pfizer going to Ireland, and Ford, Carrier and Nabisco going to Mexico. Ford is investing about 2.7 billion dollars in two plants in Mexico that expect to create about 3,800 new jobs for Mexicans, not Americans! Nabisco is moving 600 jobs to Mexico, and Carrier is moving about 1,400 jobs to Mexico. Early efforts by President Trump are an attempt to reverse this trend, and we should all hope that he will continue to be successful in keeping American jobs at home.

Just those three companies will be responsible for putting nearly 6,000 workers in this country out of a job, and that doesn't include the workers in this country who would have built the huge Ford factories and Nabisco's and Carrier's manufacturing facilities.

Pfizer's move to Ireland, called "inversion" only moves about 130 jobs, but it allows Pfizer to reduce its corporate tax rate from 35% in this country to 12.5% in Ireland. America's corporate tax rate is the highest in the industrialized world and it is costing us millions of jobs and billions of tax dollars. This is a huge problem that Washington needs to fix ASAP. The winner of the 2016 Presidential election has made that one of the top priorities for his administration.

Technology is also impacting the job markets in a very big way. Going back to the 1950s again, just about everyone had a Kodak "Brownie" box camera. These cameras were very affordable, and they took black and white pictures on rolls of Kodak film that were also reasonably priced.

Kodak became a giant company in the imaging industry. At its peak, in the 1980s, Kodak employed 62,000 people. The city of Rochester, New York was the ultimate company town. Kodak built Rochester. Today, after emerging from bankruptcy, Kodak's employment has plummeted to less than 7,000, but Rochester has survived extremely well because of the pool of talented ex-Kodak employees.

The two factors that affected Kodak so negatively were a global competitor from Japan, and the advance from analog to digital technology in the film industry. Fuji, the Japanese film and camera manufacturer, became a very aggressive competitor, and they adapted to technology changes much more quickly than Kodak.

Technology has had an enormous impact on the job markets, and this trend will continue and maybe even accelerate. It is important to understand that employers would rather employ a machine than a person if they could both do the same job at least equally well. The reason is simple. Machines represent less overhead than an employee, and overhead impacts profits.

Companies, and their management are judged and valued by the profits they can produce, and they are always looking for ways to improve efficiency and reduce expenses.

Some other contributing factors include the facts that machines don't require training, they don't take paid vacations, they don't take sick leave or maternity leave, they don't require any expensive health care benefits, they don't require managers, they don't cause political strife in their department, and they don't create turnover.

Automation, which is another word for technology, has eliminated innumerable jobs in corporate America. As the development of robotics continues, this is only going to increase. Additionally, smartphone technology has eliminated an incredible number of jobs.

Think about it. Because of your smartphone, you no longer need to buy a camera, film, or a flash attachment, and you don't need to have your pictures processed. You don't even need a video recorder. There's more:

- You don't need a watch, an alarm clock, or a stop watch.
- You don't need a dictionary or an encyclopedia.
- You don't need a calendar or an appointment book.
- You don't need a calculator.
- You don't need maps or a GPS system.
- You don't need a rolodex
- You don't need a dictation machine.
- You don't need a flashlight.
- You don't need an answering machine.
- You don't need an outdoor thermometer.
- You don't need a pedometer.
- You don't need a newspaper or a magazine.
- You don't need a radio or a television.
- You don't need a bookstore or a library.
- You don't even need a landline!

I'm sure this list isn't complete, but the point is that smartphone technology alone has eliminated the need for a very large number of products that represented volumes of jobs, especially manufacturing jobs.

This book is about helping you plan your financial survival from the time you would normally retire through the end of your life.

This chapter is about eliminating those businesses from your career plans in which you could be replaced by technology or low cost global competition.

Life has always been one big competition. It starts at a very early age. Kids in school compete for the best grades, they compete for popularity and acceptance, they compete athletically and they compete in any other way that they are being challenged.

Adults in the business world are competing every day for recognition, power and, ultimately, money. If money makes the world go around, competition is money's driving force.

Today, the competition is the fiercest it has ever been. We are not only competing with our friends and neighbors, as individuals we are competing for jobs and money globally and with technology. Some of the countries we deal with and lose volumes of jobs to, and with whom we have a huge trade deficit, like China, don't even like us, and are potentially a military threat to us. If the competition is getting fiercer, we have two choices, both as individuals and as a country: we can allow ourselves to be run over, or we can fight back.

This same scenario applies to each individual who wants to have a financially secure old age. You need to take charge and win that security. It really is survival of the fittest, and it is a competition you can't afford to lose!

CHAPTER 12

UNEMPLOYMENT, UNDEREMPLOYMENT AND LONGEVITY

A variety of studies tell us entitlements and interest on the debt account for 85% of government spending growth through the year 2024. The breakdown of this spending is:

- 32% for major health care programs

- 28% for Social Security

- 25% interest on the debt.

This makes adding any additional federal funding even more inflationary. But the most important place we need to be investing federal growth funds is in the military and national defense. At this time, the world is in chaos. We have never been surrounded by as many global hot spots as we are today, and the government needs access to more than enough money to build our military, defeat our enemies and protect our country.

You may not want to believe that money makes the world go around, but if you have ever tried to live without it, you know it's true. Unfortunately, it seems as if huge numbers of people are counting on the government to make their own world go around, both now and in the future. The unemployment rate in December of 2015 was very low at 5%. This is a result of economic gains made since the great recession.

As good as the improvement over the 2010 unemployment rate of over 10% sounds, if you use the broadest definition of employment, which includes people in this country who are 16 years of age and older who have jobs, compared to the entire 16 and older population, the Labor Department statistics show that 40.6% of the population is unemployed. Another way of explaining this is to say that the Labor Participation Rate is only 59.4%.

In October of 2015, a study done by the Social Security Administration showed that 51% of working Americans earn less than $30,000.00 a year. Sadly, 40% are earning less than $20,000.00 a year. These job participation percentages and these earnings levels do not speak well for the economic future of our country. In fact, poverty levels in this country, for the year 2015, for a family of three is reported as being $18,849.00. For a family of four, it is $24,215.00.

Remember: Sid Hydeman raised our family in the lap of luxury, without credit card debt, on a salary that never exceeded $18K in any year.

Living at these levels is oppressive! There is a lot of talk about how our kids and grandkids are going to be faced with huge challenges, but really, everyone alive today is vulnerable to this economic malaise.

The longer we live, the more vulnerable each of us becomes. We ourselves need to plan to provide the financial support that our longevity requires with the expectation that the federal government will not have the financial resources to do it for us. The unemployed and the underemployed can't count on subsidies from a country with entitlement programs that are running out of money. The 59.4% of the population that is gainfully employed, many of whom make $20,000.00 to $30,000.00 a year, can't be expected to support the 40.6% of the population that are out of the work force. And the rich can't be expected to carry more than their fair share of the burden. If the rich are taxed too heavily, they lose their incentive to risk building their companies and adding jobs. It is a vicious cycle.

There is no easy answer, but every able bodied citizen needs to do everything he or she can to protect his or her long term financial future. Longevity increases the burden of healthcare costs, not only because of the number of years that are being added, but also because the older we become, the more dependent we become on the healthcare system. Health conditions such as Alzheimer's, Parkinson's, heart disease, diabetes, cancer and others are becoming of epidemic proportion because of the aging population. Medicare is already feeling the strain, but it is quickly getting much worse. In planning for the end of our working days, we all need to factor in the real possibility that a broken government system can't support us through entitlements in our old age.

Protecting one's old age is going to take a prodigious effort that needs to be started at the earliest age possible. Many of us will live to be 90 years old and older. Supporting ourselves for all those years is the challenge each of us needs to address individually! Traditionally, Americans have considered the retirement age to be 65. If we live to be 90, we will need the means to support ourselves for twenty five years, very possibly without any government aid.

Plan for the worst, and hope for the best.

CHAPTER 13

EBSA
ENOUGH BULL STRUDEL ALREADY!

Political challenges have never been easy. Today, every problem facing our country seems even more difficult than ever before. We used to have a two party political system in this country that worked. The parties, in the past, made an effort to reach a compromise. Nobody got everything they wanted, but they arrived at a workable and mutually acceptable solution.

Today instead of having a two party system that works, America has a two party divide that can agree on practically nothing. The Democrats are considered to be politically to the left of center, and the Republicans are considered to be to the right of center. Another way many people express the differences is to call the left leaning party liberal and the right leaning party conservative. There are more registered Democrats in this country than Republicans.

The most liberal people believe that the government should take responsibility for providing equal opportunities for everyone, and it is the government's obligation to solve problems. They are considered to be the party of big government and big spending. They talk about extending entitlement programs to include universal health care. Some even believe that it is everyone's right to have free healthcare. Democrats are divided between improving the Affordable Care Act and moving to a single payer national health insurance program. The single payer health insurance plan, also known as Medicare for all, would be a system managed by a single public agency which would be responsible for the financial portion of the nation's health care. Another entitlement discussed is free public college for everyone, or at least free community college for everyone. They also discuss government programs to reduce student loan repayment. Another enormously important element of the Democrat platform is jobs. They want many more and much better paying jobs for the middle class. Additionally, they want to raise the minimum wage to $15.00 an hour.

People who have family members who are public college students or public college prospects love the idea of free college. Low income earners would love a raise to $15.00 an hour. As a humanitarian, and a compassionate person, I sympathize with those who want to provide all these wonderful benefits for all Americans.

My intention is not to be political. Instead, my goal is to protect the reader from "political bull strudel," and to offer suggestions about managing the financial challenges that most of us will face as we grow older. EBSA!

If it seems that I am picking on the liberal platform, it is simply because it is the advocate of big spending and the proponent of free entitlements for the multitudes. The conservatives are financially much more conservative than the liberals, but when it comes to bull strudel, they discuss how quickly and easily they will eliminate the crisis caused by our national debt. This problem is much too big to be managed quickly and easily. EBSA!

We've already established that money makes the world go around. If you agree with this statement, you understand that nothing of consequence in the free enterprise system is free. Someone always has to pay, and it is inevitably the taxpayer who ends up carrying the financial burden.

The free enterprise system depends on the fact that the people and companies who work in the system have the financial means and liquidity to be able to support not only themselves and their workforce, but also the ability to support sustainable economic growth.

If you believe that our government is going to provide all the benefits you will need after you turn 65, then you are counting on the government to fund your retirement. You will have, in effect, believed the political rhetoric. When you do this, you put your future, and the future of your family, in dire jeopardy.

When planning for your old age, don't believe what you hear from politicians. Believe what you can see is happening now, and recognize what has been trending in this country for over a hundred years. Realize that every trend you have read about in this book is continuing and accelerating!

Investigate things you can verify. Politicians will tell you that America is not a bankrupt nation, and politicians claim they can solve all our economic problems. Politicians say they can save Social Security and Medicare and every other entitlement program the American people would love to be able to fall back on. With what - more taxes and regulations?

Back in the early 1970's, while I was in the hospital equipment leasing business with Telco, I was in regular contact with hospital administrators. Our leases required a board resolution from the hospital's board of directors which authorized the administrator to sign our lease. While I was in Mississippi to pick up a lease, the administrator lamented to me that the hospital, for the first time had had to raise its room rate to $100.00 a night. His explanation for the increase was "government regulations" which he said were becoming more and more stringent, and were going to drive healthcare costs to being unaffordable.

Today, the average cost of a hospital room in a for profit hospital, such as his, is $1,629.00 per night.

As we all know only too well, health care and health insurance are huge political footballs. The Affordable Care Act is in the process of failing badly, and there is an effort to repeal and replace it. Getting a new healthcare bill that is politically acceptable is extremely difficult because there is no affordable, perfect solution, and different factions want different provisions. Politically, no one wants to exclude anyone from coverage, no one wants to see insurance premiums rise on an annual basis, nor does anyone want to see health care costs escalate.

All four of the powerful Big Four trends make any healthcare plan subject to serious annual insurance premium and healthcare cost escalations.

If the dollar loses buying power, the cost of healthcare must increase to offset that loss. Longevity puts a huge strain on the cost of healthcare not only because older people need more medical attention, but also because they need it for a longer period of time. Advances in medical technology improve healthcare, but they add to its cost. And the national debt accelerates inflation, which needs to be offset by increased insurance premiums and healthcare charges.

Healthcare should not be viewed as a political problem. It should be viewed as an American problem. EBSA! It's an American ECONOMIC problem. And it's an economic problem that can't be fixed by a country that is $20,000,000,000,000.00 in debt! Individually, we have to face the facts, and do whatever it takes to protect ourselves. There is no perfect, easy or inexpensive solution. In healthcare, there is no such thing as "free".

My understanding of bankruptcy is having unmanageable debt. In the previous chapter, we saw our nation's unemployment and underemployment dilemma. If we look at the national debt clock, which you can google on your smartphone at usdebtclock.org, you will see the real time numbers of our national debt. Look at them as you read this chapter. The debt clock is telling us the horrible truth. Our country, without declaring it, is in fact bankrupt, which is something no politician will admit. EBSA!

When you look at the debt clock, look at all the categories it addresses. Look not only at the national debt, but look at the unfunded liabilities, and the debt per individual, and the debt per household. As I write this book, the date is September 6th, 2016, and the national debt is $19,483,071,645,800.00. While you are reading this book, check the debt clock, and see how it has grown. The debt is out of control! Also, realize that at the same time we are paying interest on the debt, and hopefully reducing the principal, we are still funding the everyday activities of the federal government. The federal government's payroll, alone, is over 2,700,000 employees.

Additionally, and most importantly, the federal government needs to protect our citizens by more than adequately funding our national defense spending and our military! We have to be the most powerful country in the world, and the most respected, and the most feared. Those qualities will also make us the safest country in the world.

Payroll and national defense are just two major categories of government spending. There are too many other major spending categories to enumerate, and the cost and the size of these federal responsibilities continues to escalate as you have seen in the previous chapters in this book.

The Federal Government is not an income producing entity.

It is a taxing authority, and it raises money through taxation, and it borrows money by selling bonds in order to generate its working capital. Like every other entity, the Federal Government has financial limitations. If the government takes too much money from businesses and from its citizens in the form of taxes, the economy becomes stifled, jobs dry up, and people can't afford to buy and spend.

Governments, like companies and individuals, have a credit rating. The credit rating strongly influences what the government must pay, based on risk, for the money it borrows. It will become increasingly more expensive, and much more difficult for an entity like our government, which has existing debt of almost $20,000,000,000,000.00 to attract people willing to buy their bonds. Politicians' promises are made in the face of these facts. EBSA!!!

If we, as the people who need to protect our futures, believe that our country can support us in our old age, we are eating and swallowing political bull strudel! It doesn't make any difference if you are a Republican, a Democrat or an Independent if the country can't afford to fulfil political promises.

Every individual needs to think, from a political standpoint, about what makes common sense, what is practical, what is realistic, and most importantly, what is doable? Everything else is bull strudel. It is said that people vote their pocketbooks. They vote for the policies that they believe will be in their best interests economically. If the voter believes that none of the policies are realistic or achievable, it becomes apparent that the voter cannot count on the government to perform the miracles it promises. At this point, the voter needs to recognize that the only person he can count on to protect his economic future is him or herself!

Voting one's self interest is extremely important. No one else can represent you as well as you can represent yourself. However, it is equally important to vote realistically and not vote for undeliverable or unaffordable political promises. President Kennedy said it best, "Ask not what your country can do for you. Ask what you can do for your country." The best thing you can do for your country, as well as for yourself, is to become financially self-reliant. That is everyone's challenge!

CHAPTER 14

HYPOCRISY, PRACTICALITY
AND COMMON SENSE

Being open and honest, I confess I have been a gigantic beneficiary of government entitlement programs. I'm a cancer survivor, and Medicare has paid hundreds of thousands of dollars to cover chemo therapy, radiation, two surgeries and two extended hospital stays, plus home healthcare and rehab. Without Medicare, I would have been dead ten years ago, and my family would have been bankrupt. On top of that, my wife and I have been receiving Social Security since we each turned 65. In my case, that's for fifteen years, and that money has been very important to us. We also have a government insured reverse mortgage, which has eliminated our house payment in our old age which has greatly reduced our overhead and improved our cash flow.

As you've probably noticed throughout my story, "security" has always been important to me. Security was very important to me every time I considered a job in corporate America. When I was self- employed, I paid big bucks for disability and life insurance. Emotionally, and from the standpoint of being a caring human being, I would wholeheartedly support Medicare for all, which is a political initiative of one of the parties.

I wish everyone could have the availability of the government benefits that my generation has enjoyed. Unfortunately, wanting, wishing and hoping won't get it done. As much as I wish it could, as much as I want it to, and as hard as I was hoping it would, the federal government will almost surely not be able to do nearly as much for my kids, my grandkids, or members of next generations as it is doing for the current beneficiaries.

The government is drowning in debt. The entitlement programs are going broke, and politicians can't deliver on big spending policies. Common sense, which is not all that common, dictates that the government needs to cut spending, certainly not add to it, and it needs to get its financial challenges under control and back in balance.

Common sense also needs to be applied by all the individuals who are planning their financial futures. Common sense says that you need to count on yourself. Don't count on the federal government! Think of the federal government as a gigantic Continental Can Company. Continental Can conscientiously tried to do everything for its employees. Continental Can went broke for trying. The federal government is on exactly the same path.

The federal government has lots of financial responsibilities to the taxpayers. The first and foremost priority is to protect us militarily. The direction the world is moving represents big and multiple threats to our homeland security.

The government can't do it all. Each individual needs to plan to protect his or her own long term well being. The timing of that planning and the timing of implementing that plan is crucial to the plan's success. Everyone who hasn't started needs to start as immediately as possible. Time is your ally. The more time you have to manage your financial future, the better.

Governments are just like corporations or individuals. The rich countries are like rich people and rich corporations are powerful because they have the money to do powerful things. Poor countries, poor people and poor corporations become powerless because they don't have the money to live up to extravagant promises. Our federal government's entitlement programs are much too rich for a country so burdened by debt.

Political common sense needs to be the party of your future. If it's true that voters vote their pocketbooks, the best way to vote your pocketbook is to take charge of your own financial future, no matter what the politicians are promising.

EBSA!!

CHAPTER 15

TIMING

Time is an ally, and the more time you have to implement a plan, the better the plan should be. However, time has a characteristic that needs to be recognized and respected. This characteristic is known as a "cycle." It seems that every business is vulnerable to cycles. In the real estate business the adage has been "location, location, location." I agree that location is extremely important, but I think that "timing" is equally important.

Timing is not only important in real estate, it is important in almost every business decision that people make on a daily basis.

**Every business success I achieved was
because my timing was good.
Every business failure I suffered was
because my timing was bad.**

Continental Can would have been a great employer if I had been hired at the right time, which would have been years before. Telco would have been a great success if interest rates hadn't spiked to an all-time high at the time the company was emerging. Being a banker or a real estate executive in Dallas, and owning or lending on or brokering prime properties was being in a great place at the right time until the S&L crisis hit. It has since become a great place again.

It seems that every business is vulnerable to cycles. Today, even the price of oil is spiraling down. Oil has been over $135.00 a barrel. Recently, it went under $30.00 a barrel. People in the oil business, and lenders in the oil business, while this trend continues, are going through a very bad cycle.

It is extremely hard to time a cycle properly because when things are going well, people become euphoric and believe the good times will never end, and when things are bottoming out of a bad cycle, people are cautious because they don't think things will ever be good again. When cycles overheat, they form a "bubble," and when that bubble breaks, the cycle can go from being overly hot to overly cold in an instant! The key to playing the cycles is to get in early and get out early. Take your profits and run. Don't be afraid of leaving money on the table.

**Speaking from more experience than I'd like to admit,
I was great at getting in, but lousy at getting out.**

Greed and being overly optimistic can be devastating. When things turn cold, they become unsaleable unless the seller is willing to sell at a big discount from a normal market. Every investment including the stock market, commodities, real estate and even monetary metals go through cycles. It only takes one good ride to make things right, but remember: Buy low and sell high! You don't go broke taking profits.

You can't win if you don't take the risk of playing. Capitalism is about taking risks to achieve rewards. Just be smart and understand how to protect yourself on the downside. Smart is a component of being lucky or good. The smarter you are the better and luckier you will become!

CHAPTER 16

BETTING YOUR FUTURE ON A COMPANY

I spoke about the effect of timing a few pages back. It also affects what used to be known as "fringe benefits", which didn't really even exist until the 1930s. With very few exceptions, most people worked either on their own farms or operated their own small companies. There was no income tax until 1913, and retirement wasn't really considered necessary. People worked until their health failed or until they died. As the nation moved from an agrarian society to a more corporatized society, the need to attract skilled, talented employees led businesses to offer features like paid vacation time, retirement, health insurance, and more in addition to financial compensation. Over time, the word "fringe" disappeared as benefits were considered a standard part of employment. When I entered the workforce, it was considered a mark of prestige to be hired by a company who invested in such total well being of its employees. Despite the good intentions of companies, however, the financial burden of bearing ever-increasing costs has driven many to closing or bankruptcy. Benefits are becoming "fringe" again. The cycle of providing cradle-to-grave care for employees has essentially concluded.

Hefty fringe benefits make companies very vulnerable to being over extended. When a company's overhead gets too high, it needs to raise its prices to cover that overhead. When this happens, these companies find themselves unable to compete with companies that have much leaner overhead, and, consequently, lower sales prices. This eventually puts the top heavy company out of business.

Corporate health care plans alone are extremely heavy overhead, but retirement plans on top of health care become corporate killers as the number of retirees grows over time. Back when retirement plans were first introduced, salaries were lower, the number of employees was lower, and longevity was shorter. Early on, when an employee retired at age 65, they often died within five years of retirement. This made their retirement affordable for the employer.

Many of America's biggest, oldest and most successful companies have filed for bankruptcy because of their pension liabilities. Some, like Chrysler and General Motors, have survived bankruptcy because of government bailouts, but many big name, very established companies, that didn't have government support, didn't make it. Today, corporate security is pretty much a thing of the past. Instead of relying on corporate retirement plans and healthcare plans, employees contribute to or totally fund their own benefits.

Most companies no longer have formal training programs for the people they hire right out of college the way Continental Can trained me. There is a good reason why they don't. The year I was hired, Continental Can hired and trained fifty four college graduates across all their divisions. If the company spent $50,000.00 per trainee, as they said they did, their investment in that group was $2,700,000.00.

Because I had been in the service twice, I hadn't been aware of what was happening with my class of trainees during my absence. As it turned out, I was the last person from my training class still with the company. The others had all been hired away by the competition for much more money because they had been well trained and were field ready. No one in my class stayed with Continental Can for more than six years.

Continental Can and other big companies like it
were funding the training for their competition.

The job market, and employee attitudes have changed enormously. Today most people in the job market expect to change jobs on a regular basis. Employers plan to keep their employees only as long as they are productive and affordable. Loyalty is a thing of the past, and both the employer and the employee are only concerned with their own self interests. Income to the employee, and profits to the corporation are the driving forces.

Everyone needs to be looking out for number one. This is especially true about retirement. No one can count on anyone but themselves to fund their long term retirement. This is going to be a huge challenge! I have personally experienced, and we've all seen how major corporations have suffered and failed trying to provide "security" for their employees.

The federal government is going through the same process.

Social Security, which is a godsend to many Americans, will eventually go broke. By some reports, the most recent estimate is that Social Security will run out of money by 2034. One extremely important thing about Social Security that everyone needs to understand is that it is not, by itself, a comfortable retirement income. Even if it NEVER runs out of money, Social Security will never allow you to live securely on your monthly benefit alone. To live comfortably in retirement, you are going to need significant additional income. Medicare, also a godsend, is projected by many to be out of money by 2026, even sooner than Social Security.

Our federally funded "entitlement programs" are doing to our government the same things that corporate fringe benefits have done to many of our mature major corporations.

Our national debt is over $19,000,000,000,000.00 as of 2016. There are roughly 323,000,000 Americans. If you divide our national debt by the number of Americans, the amount that each of us owes, including babies who are born today, is $59,375.00. And this number is growing by the minute.

On top of this, it is estimated that we have $123,000,000,000,000.00 in unfunded liabilities for just three entitlement programs. (Yes, that is TRILLION) These three programs are Social Security, Medicare and the Medicare Prescription Drug Program.

The debt for unfunded liabilities per person is $381,597.75 as of March 10th, 2016, and growing by the minute.

A recent survey discovered that 62% of Americans have less than $1,000.00 in savings. One third of that number have no savings at all. My understanding of the simple definition of bankruptcy is having more debt than you can manage. If you accept this definition, our country, without declaring it, is bankrupt!

MY THEN AND NOW

At the end of Section I. I detailed real life examples of how the buying power of the dollar had eroded during my father's lifetime. So far, during my lifetime, the erosion of the buying power of the dollar has accelerated.

An extreme example is the house I paid $20,300.00 for in 1964.

- I sold the house in 1969 for $36,500.00.
- I made a very nice, 75%, profit in four and a half years.
- Since then, the attic has been renovated to include a fourth bedroom and a second bathroom.
- On the internet, the home is now shown to be 1,493 square feet. Zillow has estimated its current value to be $1,379,818.00

- The house has increased in value by 68 times what I paid for it just 52 years ago.
- As I mentioned, my mortgage on that house was $104.25 a month.
- Today, in my present home, my water bill is often over $200.00 a month.

The prices on the house reflect some real appreciation, but water doesn't appreciate much. The biggest reason for the price increases, excluding supply and demand, is the erosion of the buying power of the dollar.

The bad news is that the debt that
overhangs our country will accelerate
as the deterioration of the dollar's buying power continues.

The value of the dollar is not only affected by its buying power, but it is also affected by its earning power. As mentioned earlier, back in the 1960's, saving rates were 5% and C.D.'s could earn 6%. Today with the government holding interest rates artificially low, savings accounts are paying about 1% and C.D.'s earn about 1.25%.

For years we have been told to save for retirement. Now that many of us are retired the government has destroyed the earning power of the money we saved! So, retirees face the cruel, hard facts that their money buys less and earns less. Retirees are also challenged by the fact that due to longevity their money with low buying power and low earning power is going to have to last them for what will hopefully be a very long time.

The financial ability to retire, for the vast majority of us, is, and certainly will increasingly continue to be, out of reach.

CHAPTER 17

MONEY AND SUBSTANCE

On June 5th, 1933, President Franklin D. Roosevelt took the United States currency off the gold standard. While we were on the gold standard, paper dollars were redeemable for gold dollars. Simply stated, if you had a twenty dollar bill, you were entitled to exchange it evenly for a twenty dollar gold piece. Today, if you wanted to exchange twenty dollar bills for a twenty dollar gold piece, you would need forty nine of them. Twenty dollar gold pieces currently sell for about $980.00.

While we were on the gold standard,
our currency was backed by things of substance.

Gold and silver are known as "monetary metals." Our dimes, quarters, half dollars and silver dollars were made of silver.

The larger denominations of money, starting at $2.50, known as a quarter eagle, were made of gold. A $5.00, half eagle, a $10.00, eagle, and a $20.00, double eagle were in circulation from around 1795 until 1933. In spite of the fact that the gold standard had been abandoned in 1933, the government maintained a dollar to gold relationship at $35.00 an ounce until August 15th, 1971. At that time, the dollar's link to gold was completely severed by President Richard Nixon.

Abandoning the gold standard has proven to be a gigantic mistake. Today, the different denominations of American dollar bills are known as "federal reserve notes." Instead of being supported by the value of monetary metals which are things of real substance, Federal Reserve notes are backed only by "the good faith and credit of the government of the United States."

When the United States government lowers the earning power of the dollar by artificially lowering interest rates on savings accounts and certificates of deposit, which dramatically hurts savers, especially seniors who need the retirement income, and who have been saving for many years, it is showing bad faith.

And, when the United States government accumulates $19,000,000,000,000,000.00 in debt, and that debt is growing, and the country is technically bankrupt, its credit rating is questionable at best! The federal government has the power of the printing press, and since money today is only paper, with nothing of substance backing it, they can print a lot of money. The problem with printing paper money is that it doesn't increase economic activity; it just causes inflation.

Inflation devalues the buying power of the dollar, so if a person is retired and living on a fixed income, inflation is the equivalent of an economic demotion. History has shown us what inflation has done in the past, and if history is the "great teacher" it is reputed to be, the value of the dollar is in for a very rough ride. The first time my father's house doubled in value, it went from $13,750.00 to $27,500.00. The next time it doubles, it will go from being worth about $1,750,000 to about $3,500,000.00. Can you imagine how much paper money you will have to earn to buy this house in the future?

To make matters much worse, the incredible debt overhanging our economy will accelerate these inflationary numbers. Confidence in the value of our money has declined significantly since we abandoned the gold standard. Federal Reserve notes don't hold their value nearly as well as currency tied to something of substance such as monetary metals.

Gold and silver are important components for any retirement account, not because they will beat inflation, but because they will stabilize the account's buying power against inflation. As the buying power of the dollar declines, the value of monetary metals increases, thus protecting the buying power of a person's retirement account.

CHAPTER 18

THE VALUE OF THE ENTREPRENEUR

Politicians in both parties talk about creating jobs. Some politicians also demand higher wages for the workers who have jobs. Jobs imply employment. You need an employer to have a job, and if you have an employer, you work at the discretion of that employer. You don't control your own destiny. Some jobs are dead ends. They have little or no upside potential. Don't let yourself settle for a job with no future. The best jobs are jobs that offer the opportunity to build and grow your personal future irrespective of how well or poorly your employer's business does.

If you have an opportunity, rather than just a job, you can create your own value without depending on the government to get you a raise. When evaluating a job with an opportunity, determine if you think it is an opportunity you would want to pursue for the rest of your life, and if it is a business that lends itself to being replicated or improved by someone like yourself.

Becoming an entrepreneur is great job security. You can rest assured that you are not going to get fired, and you can bet that no one is going to lay you off because you are too old or too expensive. Another great thing about being a successful entrepreneur is that you have an asset that can be sold at a value based on the income the business generates, or you can pass the business on to family members.

There is another huge advantage to being an entrepreneur. Instead of being the employee, you become the boss. Entrepreneurs are the backbones of capitalism and small business in America. They are also the biggest factor in job creation in the country.

Instead of only encouraging job creation and higher wages, politicians need to differentiate between jobs and opportunities, and encourage people to become entrepreneurs, high income earners, and ultimately employers.

By encouraging more entrepreneurs, politicians will have helped generate many more jobs. Having employees gives the employer the advantage of having leverage which is an important tool. With leverage, the employer is making income on not only his own efforts, but also on the efforts of his income producing employees. This is extremely important in looking at long term retirement. The employer can hire people to run his business and make him money no matter how old the business owner becomes.

Another fabulous tool in building long term financial security is residual income. In most sales situations, the seller makes money only at the time he consummates his sale. He has to work very hard to keep making sales on an everyday basis.

RESIDUAL INCOME

Residual income is income that repeats itself after the initial business has been conducted. A perfect example of residual income is rental income on real estate. If you own a rental property and sign a three year lease with your tenant, you will receive thirty six payments, not just one.

At the end of three years, if the market will support it, you can renegotiate the lease for more money, or find another tenant. This allows you to stay current with inflation. Another huge advantage to this kind of income is that the tenant is paying off your mortgage and you are building equity. The way to leverage real estate is to buy more rental properties.

Selling insurance policies is another very powerful way to generate residual income. You get paid monthly as the insurance company receives its premiums. In this case, you don't have to invest to receive residual cash flow. Obviously, not every business opportunity throws off residual income, but it is something to be aware of and hopefully an idea you can incorporate to your advantage.

NOTHING IS SMOOTH OR EASY

There are big risks and heartburn in becoming an entrepreneur and a business owner. Most people need to borrow money to go into business for themselves. Bank loans are a risk. As your business grows, you have to be willing to hire and fire people.

Hiring people requires a payroll, and things like office space, office furniture, and office equipment such as computers and telephones among other things. An entrepreneur also needs an attorney to protect his legal interests, and an accountant to manage his taxes. And an employer has a lot of responsibility for the well being of his employees. Firing people is emotionally stressful, and the way people litigate these days, it can become a legal nightmare.

Entrepreneurs take the risk of failure. Harry Truman's famous line was, "If you can't stand the heat, get out of the kitchen." If you are risk averse, then you probably would be very uncomfortable being an entrepreneur.

But, if you are willing to trade the risk for the potential of unlimited rewards, being an entrepreneur can be very exciting. It can also be a long hard roller coaster ride, but it only takes one success to make the risks and frustrations much more than worthwhile.

**If you don't swing the bat, you might take a walk,
but you'll never hit a homerun.**

The most important thing to remember is that, somehow, each individual needs a path to financial survival, and that path needs to be as long as a lifetime. In later chapters, I am going to explain some options for your consideration which may help you make the best decision for yourself.

Make no mistake: You need to answer your own questions, and you need to start doing so right now!

CHAPTER 19

WHAT'S THE REAL TRUTH?

Politicians, financial planners, investment advisers, and everyone else who has a vested interest in telling their listeners all the good things they can do for them regarding a comfortable retirement, are painting pretty pictures that will be very hard to deliver on.

The picture I've presented of my family's story is 'painted by numbers', and unfortunately, the numbers don't lie. Our 100 year personal history depicts practical American history starting in 1913, and it shows the trend of what has happened to the buying power, and the earning power of the dollar over the last hundred years.

With the national debt, and the unfunded liabilities that overhang our economy, the negative trend we've witnessed for the dollar has the potential to become like a locomotive going downhill without brakes. We could be looking at the biggest economic bubble in the history of the world. All the pieces are in place for that to happen. The federal government doesn't just have to pay down our national debt, it also needs to raise the money to run the country on a daily basis. The size and overhead of our government is astronomical. Its payroll alone, as mentioned earlier, is over 2,700,000 people before it does anything or spends anything.

When I graduated from college in 1959, even though I had majored in Government, I chose not to work for the government because private sector compensation was much more attractive. Recently, a Cato Institute study showed that government compensation is now 78% better than private sector income. According to this study, when adding in benefits pay, federal employees earned, on average, $119,934.00, while private sector workers earned $67,246.00. The difference is $52,688.00. Cato based this study on figures provided by the U.S. Bureau of Economic Analysis, the BEA. If you multiply the number of employees by the average earnings of government employees, the government payroll alone is $326,220,480,000.00. This is extremely cumbersome and enormously expensive.

In spite of this, the one area where we absolutely need to increase spending significantly is in the rebuilding of our military. We are surrounded by enemies all over the world who would love to destroy us. Some of them are terrorist organizations like Isis and AL Qaeda, and some of them have nuclear weapons like Russia, China and North Korea. Iran is the largest active state sponsor of terrorism and its leadership encourages "death to America." This is not a complete list, but it explains why our military and our homeland security need to be a major funding priority. If we can't defend ourselves, we become sitting ducks for our enemies.

The simple question is, "Where does the money come from?" The answer is "From you, the taxpayer."

So, it is easy to see that any political platform that promises free college, and Medicare for all, and any other government giveaway program, is probably unaffordable and likely an insult to the intelligence of the voting public.

Our country needs to work toward fiscal responsibility because if we don't have a financially responsible government, our monetary system will become unstable, and our civilization, as we have known it, will be in jeopardy. This is a worst case scenario, and the extreme opposite of political "happy talk," but it needs to be included in our thinking about the future.

Historically, great civilizations have come and gone. Ours is the greatest civilization of all time, but each of us must do our part to make sure that our economy flourishes and our way of life survives. Putting too much financial pressure on the already fragile government by being financially dependent on it to fund our long term well being will destroy capitalism and the free enterprise system.

The onus is on us!

CHAPTER 20

DOES FREE ENTERPRISE WORK?

The Federal Government of the Unites States is not in the business of making money. It is not and never has been a for profit entity. The way the government generates its cash receivables is by taxing the profits and income earned by corporations and individuals. The Federal Government is what is known as a "taxing authority."

As we saw earlier, only about 60% of the population over the age of 16 is producing income, and there are many in the workforce who pay little or no taxes. This results in the government depending on higher income earners to pay a very disproportional amount of the burden of funding the government. As the debt and the unfunded liabilities grow, the tax receivables have to be increased in order to fund all the government's responsibilities.

Somewhere, somehow, something has to give. The corporations and individuals who are paying taxes can't support all the things for which the government has accepted responsibility. Remember, these taxpayers are the same group who need to have enough after-tax cash flow and profit to be able to provide the jobs, and even the new jobs, that everyone is screaming for.

They need to be able to grow their businesses without worrying that the government could cripple them with taxes. People who favor big government need to realize that the taxpayers who are funding the government are way overextended and cannot continue much longer to support all the entitlement programs that are drowning in red ink. These are the same people who are competing globally with international companies where taxes are much lower.

Many people recognize the problem. Everybody wants a solution, and politicians claim they have answers that can be quickly instituted to overcome the challenges. But numbers have never lied, and no country has ever faced financial challenges with numbers as large as ours.

The numbers dictate that we dramatically reduce the size of the federal government in every area except national defense and the military which need to be enhanced in every way possible. The federal government needs to delegate everything it can to the states, and the states need to delegate everything they can to more local government.

As things stand today, it seems as if everything needs federal government approval. This takes times and costs money. This is great for lawyers and accountants, but it makes doing business much too difficult. During the Obama administration alone, over 20,000 new regulations have been put on the books. While we know America is a country of laws, it is now pretty clear that America is a country of too many laws and regulations.

In the late 1950's, when I was a government major in college, it was explained that two major economic ideologies were Communism and the Free Enterprise System. Under a Communist regime, the government owns and controls everything including every individual's income. In a Free Enterprise System, businesses are owned, either publicly by stockholders, or privately by individuals, and each person is paid based on his or her market value or value to the company.

We were told that over the course of time, because government control in Communism was so effective, the regime would continuously be able to loosen restrictions. We were also told that as corporations and individuals in the Free Enterprise System took unfair advantage of the system, more and more regulations would be imposed to control those violations. It was projected that, at some point in time, the two ideologies would meet in the middle. At the time this seemed incomprehensible. Today, nearly 60 years later, it seems to be approaching reality.

Regulations are destroying the Free Enterprise System and it is becoming more and more difficult to do business in this country. This is happening at a time when we need millions of good paying jobs, and at a time that our global competitors are taking every advantage of our inability to respond to market conditions and compete effectively.

This is not intended to sound political. The only political position that this book endorses is the position of truth, realism, common sense and supportability. As a humanitarian, I wish that everyone could have not only everything they need, but also everything they want. That would make this a more perfect world. Unfortunately, right now, the world is much closer to chaos than it is to perfection. This is a very hard statement to make, but it is an easy observation. We see chaos via the media every day from all over the world, including religious related terror, racially related unrest and political protests in our own country.

As mentioned, the government gets its money from the taxpayers, and it then redistributes the money according to its priorities and its ability to fund those priorities. The Big Four I've listed at the beginning of this section strongly suggest that Social Security and Medicare are fast becoming too much of a burden to be supportable long term. The Big Four explain, from a real world perspective, why I can't believe that expansive entitlement policies are realistic, affordable, or in the best interests of a country with an economy based on the Free Enterprise System for very much longer.

Don't bet your retirement on government entitlements. Bet on yourself and common sense, and if the government is there to help you, that will be a great bonus. Everything else is bull strudel.

CHAPTER 21

THE IMPORTANCE OF CONTACT CAPITAL

Since I can't know my readers personally, I can't possibly give them individualized, personal advice. Instead, I've written this book to explain WHY, not HOW, each individual needs to start preparing to support himself or herself throughout their lifetime. All I can do is offer some general insights, gained from experience, that might open the door to opportunities that the reader may not have been aware of, or considered.

Since each of us has different educational, personal and professional backgrounds, each of us needs to factor our experience and our interests into our long term financial solution. No matter who you are or what you have done, the most important thing you can do is to create and bank as many personal and professional relationships as you can accumulate. These relationships represent Contact Capital. Everybody you know may at some point become important to your financial future. You never know who or when. Treat everyone as if they are very important, not only because they are and it's the right thing to do, but because a good personal relationship could lead to a great business opportunity.

This is not meant to suggest that you should use friendships to your selfish advantage. Business relationships need to be good for both parties or they won't work or survive. Contact Capital implies that you create relationships with people whom you can help, and who can help you.

IT'S NOT WHAT YOU KNOW, IT'S WHO YOU KNOW.

Make it a point to surround yourself with people who can help you succeed. This may sound self-promotional, but by being surrounded by powerful people, you become a center of influence and you gain the power to help others succeed. As an aside, if you don't promote yourself, don't expect anyone else to promote you. It isn't going to happen.

If you know the right people, you can make money together. This is an extremely important concept known as "networking." Nobody can do business with everybody, but everybody can do business with somebody.

Contact Capital is people power and if you are willing to make the effort to meet the right people, you can become unstoppable. Creating Contact Capital is a lifelong pursuit. You never know how important the next person you meet could be to your future.

Recently, I called the friend who had, twenty-five years ago, urged me to consider becoming an independent distributor in his organization. (You will see this story in the next chapter.) His wife answered the phone, and when I asked her how everything was going, her answer surprised me. She said, "We just got home from Costco. I hate Costco!" I asked her why she hated Costco, and her answer surprised me again. She said that she saw lots of things at Costco that they needed, but her husband wouldn't allow her to buy any of them. She went on to say that "there is no money in this household."

When her husband got on the phone, I mentioned an opportunity that I thought might help solve their financial problem. It was his turn to surprise me with his answer. He said, "I don't know anybody any more. I don't know who is dead or alive."

It was apparent that he had given up, and had allowed himself to lose all his "contact capital." His wife and he are now totally dependent on their Social Security income, which is, at best, a challenge and a struggle!

Remember what Winston Churchill said about never, never, never giving up, don't let yourself do it!! Also, remember the adage that "Quitters never win, and winners never quit!"

Staying solvent can be a lifelong challenge.

Remember the earlier quote by Winston Churchill, and amend it to "Never, never, never give up building your Contact Capital."

Continue to make yourself very available to new friends. This will open the door to big dividends!

Chapter 22

WHAT NOW

Think back to where I was at the end of Section I. After having been disabled for the best part of five years, and after making every effort to find a job, it became apparent that I was swimming upstream against a very strong current. I was burned out of real estate, and I was looking for a brand new direction in which I had no training, no experience and no contact capital! All my contact capital had been in the real estate business. After the S&L Crisis in Dallas, many of my contacts had gone off in different directions. When you are out of touch for five years, it is hard to rekindle a business relationship. People often feel that they have moved on from you. I learned firsthand what happens when you neglect that contact capital!

I was really starting all over from scratch.

You don't want to be where I was. I was 58 years old, unemployable, broke, and one of my kids was still in an expensive private university. Additionally, I needed to feed, clothe and provide shelter for my wife and myself. Things were looking very dismal!

Remember that old friend from the last chapter? The one who I said had introduced me to direct sales? Out of the blue, having heard of my plight, he had called to discuss a business opportunity. My friend had been the president of a division of one of the major banks in Dallas that had failed during the S&L Crisis. He was a little older than I was, and he had encountered a similar problem in finding a good job.

His solution to the employment problem was to become an independent distributor in a direct sales company. One of the advantages of being an independent distributor is that you don't have to compete for a job. All you need to do is find someone who is willing to sponsor you into the business. This is very easy, because whoever sponsors you earns overrides on your business.

Additionally, your sponsor has no liability for your actions. He is in no way your employer or your boss. Being an independent distributor means that you own your distributorship, and you are in business for yourself. You are now your own boss.

I wanted a job with a salary and fringe benefits and all the perks, and I kept declining my friend's offer. One evening, after I had received a number of job rejections, my friend asked me a dirty question. He asked me, "What do you have to do that's better?" He had me right where he wanted me. I signed up in his organization the next morning.

I started my distributorship with trepidation, but I quickly realized, to my amazement, that there are many, many benefits to being an independent distributor. To begin with, the cost to buy my distributorship and be in business for myself, including product to use for myself, to use as samples and to sell, was only about $1,000.00.

As you may remember, in my real estate days, during the good times, I had ten sales associates, and three in staff. My overhead was $30,000.00 a month. My risk in the real-estate business was $360,000.00 a year before I took a dime in profit, and my profits were earned from the production of only ten associates for whom I was fully liable.

It was quickly apparent to me that in direct sales my risk was hugely reduced, and my profits could be generated by an unlimited number of people for whom I had no liability. The risk to reward ratio was greatly in my favor.

In a conventional business, sales associates are supposed to make the ownership money, and staff members cost the ownership money. Everyone is on the payroll, and they all create overhead.

In a direct sales company, most independent distributors work out of their homes, and they have no staff and no payroll.

Additionally, instead of having ten income-producing associates as I did in the real estate business, a hard working independent distributor can have thousands or even tens of thousands of independent associates making him money with a minimum of overhead.

The reason independent distributors have no payroll is because the company does all the fulfilment of product, and they have every transaction credited to each of the distributors on the company computer.

The company pays each distributor, based on his or her performance, on a pre-determined schedule, usually weekly or monthly, and most often, the payment is made electronically by direct deposit into the distributor's checking account.

You don't even need to walk to your mailbox to get paid.

One of the really great things about being an independent distributor is that it answers very important questions for many entrepreneurs. The questions are, "What am I going to sell, how can I afford the inventory, and will I need employees?"

There's an easy answer to each question: Find a sponsor who represents a company that has a line of products that you can enthusiastically take to market. Your product line is everything the company you have chosen to represent has for sale.

As far as inventory goes, an independent distributor needs very little. Having enough product to be able to use for yourself, and to provide samples and sell to prospective associates is important, but the company ships its inventory directly to all your customers.

Being a "product of your product" is very important. That just means that you are not only selling the product, you are also an enthusiastic user of the product.

An important consideration about the products is that they are consumable. In order to make a consistent monthly income, you want your customer base to need to reorder product every month. This can be accomplished by placing an automatic monthly order to be filled by the company.

It is very important that you really like and respect your sponsor because he or she will be an important asset to your company and yourself for as long as you are in the business.

Because your sponsor makes overrides on the sales your organization makes, that person has a serious vested interest in helping your organization be as successful as possible. There is a saying in the direct sales industry that "you are in business for yourself, but not by yourself." Your sponsor, and the people above your sponsor need you to do well because you contribute to their income and success. They will help and support your efforts.

You never need to hire a sales force, and unless you become enormously successful, you will never need employees. Remember, the people you sponsor in the business are independent distributors just like yourself, and they will be building a network of distributors whose sales will be earning you a monthly or weekly override. This is the leveraged, residual income that can create the cash flow that can outlast a lifetime.

There is a huge difference between a conventional business, and a direct sales marketing business. Both types of businesses represent an opportunity to build success, but the starting points are totally different.

In a conventional business, most people, depending on education and experience, start at or near the bottom. It is their challenge to climb the corporate ladder and get as close to the top of their corporate entity as their talent and infighting ability allows. These people are all employees, and they face tremendous competition and political challenges on their way up the ladder. They are also fighting for pay raises in a company that can only afford raises based on the company's success and its budget.

In a direct sales company, the independent distributor starts at the top of his or her organization. He or she is starting at the top of a one person company. It then becomes that person's challenge to build his organization, below him, as big as he can, without limitation! Because an independent distributor has no payroll, he has no budget which would limit his ability to grow the number of people in his organization who can earn him an unlimited weekly or monthly income.

The first step is to find a great sponsor in a company which has products about which you can be extremely excited and which you think will attract a broad volume of customers and new distributors.

Secondly, investigate the company's management and financial capabilities. Start-ups are fine if the management is strong and if the company is not undercapitalized. If you are concerned about the company's long term viability, find one that you think is more stable. Ideally, the longevity of your company needs to equal your longevity!

Thirdly investigate the product line to be sure that the products have a great story, and one that can't easily be replicated or sold at a big discount to your company's selling price.

Lastly, investigate the company's compensation plan. There are two ways to build a sales organization, you can build it wide or you can build it deep.

Building wide means that you need to personally sponsor a certain number of people. For example, if you personally bring five people into your organization, your business would be described as being "five wide." Another way of saying this is to say you have five "legs."

There are some excellent direct sales companies that have compensation plans that require their reps to build wide, and these companies usually only pay two or three levels deep. In these companies, the distributors have to keep building wider and wider in order to keep their business viable.

From a long term perspective, with the idea that this income needs to last well into your old age, knowing by then you don't want to have to keep working intensely, finding a company with a compensation plan that emphasizes paying deep makes a lot of sense.

Just about every direct sales company has its own variation of a compensation plan, and usually, there are additional ways to create income which complement the primary part of the pay plan.

I have seen pay plans that have as many as seven different ways a distributor can earn money.

These pay plans can be very complicated and confusing. Usually, complicated and confusing means that there are multiple ways to get paid, and that is a very good thing.

The best way to attack a pay plan is to keep it very simple. The only thing you need to know is what you need to do next during each step of the way in order to continuously build your business. Just concentrate on the present and learn what you need to do next when you get there.

Your sponsor and people in your organization will be happy to explain everything you need to know to be successful because your success adds to their success.

Your business is both a sprint and a marathon. You want to go as fast as you can, but you also want to keep building for as long as you can. This is why you want to start a soon as you can. People with "contact capital," people with technology skills and people who work hard and smart can become financially independent in a few years, and they can build their business much bigger from there.

Don't believe that this is going to be easy. This is a people intensive business. In the beginning, new distributors are going to need a great deal of up line support. Also, this kind of business has a very high failure rate. You are going to want to keep building in order to find leaders who can continue to help you build even deeper. It is these new leaders who will make you rich.

Don't allow yourself to be one of those failures! Work with your sponsor and the people you have sponsored in a teamwork like effort to make everyone successful. Determination, commitment and smart, hard work can create a pot of gold at the end of the rainbow!

Be sure to know that there are absolutely no glass ceilings. The computer does not discriminate against anyone. There is no way to tell who is going to be great or who is going to fail. Everyone who wants a chance deserves a chance. The lifestyle a direct sales opportunity offers is much less regimented than a conventional business lifestyle. If you enjoy travel, you can go to any country in which your company does business and recruit distributors in that country.

In spite of the fact that this is a home based business, it can become a global business. Travel is done at your expense, since you won't have a company expense account, but you are entitled to tax deductions for your business expenses. Ask a tax advisor about the tax benefits of a home based business, as there are a number of them.

If you like the idea of investing in a direct sales business of your own, do not procrastinate! Procrastination costs you time, and lost time costs money. Make an intelligent decision. But make it quickly and decisively!

Direct sales is definitely not for everyone. You may have a much better idea for yourself based on your background and experience, and you may already have the financial backing and business savvy to follow that path. The key thing is to do something that will make you successful and allow you to be financially responsible through the rest of your life.

CHAPTER 23

STRAIGHT TALK

People read business books with the hope that the author will give them specific answers to specific questions. Readers want solutions. I can't deliver that. You are a product of your own background, education, and personal experiences. You will need to use your personal history in order to determine the best solution to your long term financial security. Telling my story is my attempt to provide insight into the trends that will affect everyone's ability to successfully navigate, financially, through an extended lifetime.

You know that "experience is the best teacher." Learning from experience can be a very tough way to learn, and an extremely expensive experience. If reading my experiences as contrasted to those of my father, helps you avoid some of those painful and expensive experiences, then I will have succeeded.

It is human nature to be optimistic, and no one wants to think negatively about their future. People have the tendency to think in the present and let the future take care of itself. Sadly, the future gets here in a hurry, and it definitely doesn't take care of itself.

My shot across your bow is screaming at you to pay attention and, starting right now, to wake up to the real world! Age 65 today is very much younger than it used to be. People used to retire at 65 because they were near the end of their lives and had become too old to be productive. Today, 65 year-olds not only have a lot of life left to live, they are still very capable. They also have a lot of experience to fall back on. You can't afford to wait until you are 65 before you address the financial needs of the rest of your life.

Like everyone else who reads this book, you will need to figure out for yourself where your time can most effectively and profitably be spent in order to insure continuity of income and lifestyle after age 65.

Chapter 24

MORE STRAIGHT TALK

This book is for you and about you, but it uses the Hydeman business experiences spanning 100 years in order for you to more clearly see your future. My comments about direct sales are based on my personal experience in this space. I would not be able to speak with any authority about direct sales if I had no experience in it.

I have been an independent distributor with one company for over 24 years, and I have made a comfortable living in this business. At the age of 80, the cash flow from this company, although it is slowly declining, continues to be an important part of my monthly income. But remember, during some of this time, my wife and I also had well over $30,000.00 a year in Social Security income as well as having received many hundreds of thousands of dollars in Medicare benefits.

I wish this kind of cash flow and these kinds of benefits for everyone who needs them, and, in the future, I expect that will be most of us. The problem is, because of our country's financial condition, the government may not be able to live up to its part of the bargain, and if we as individuals don't take responsibility for our own wellbeing, we could find ourselves up a nasty creek without a paddle!

There are many people who will tell you that direct sales is not their thing. That is exactly what I told my friend who introduced me to the industry. There are also many people who have tried and failed who say that being in a direct sales business didn't work for them. One thing I have learned for sure is that there are no free rides. As a business owner, you have to work hard for your business and make it a success before you can expect your business to work for you.

I thoroughly agree that nothing is for everyone. As mentioned earlier, I can't know you, so I certainly can't know what is best for you, but I am convinced that the future is going to require most of us to have an independent income from the age of 65 or earlier through the end of their life.

A realistic alternative to not having an income, if there are no government subsidies, is starvation.

I would ask the people who don't think direct sales is "their thing" the same question I was asked in 1994 when I was facing starvation: What do you have to do that is better?

It is my belief that direct sales is a fabulous solution for millions of people who don't yet know much about it, don't realize the need for it, but for whom it could open the door to great things.

If you want to build an organization, some great prospects include business professionals such as doctors, dentists, lawyers, accountants, restaurant and retail owners, life insurance salespeople, bartenders, hairdressers and barbers, and really, just about everyone else who is willing to make a commitment to being successful.

These professionals all have contact capital. Their patients and their customers will all need a long term, leveraged, residual income, and by sharing an opportunity like this with the people in his or her center of influence, that person is doing the people he has a relationship with a big favor.

As an example, dentists stand on their feet and look in people's mouths all day. This gets harder and harder to do the older they get, not only for the dentist, but especially for his patients. No one wants an old blind dentist with shaky hands doing a root canal. But dentists, while they are practicing, are a fabulous center of influence, with built-in contact capital. Dentists don't want to be practicing dentistry into their old age, but they are going to want the assurance of leveraged, residual cash flow that can last a lifetime. Dentists are just an example, but they are an example that a smart independent distributor can extend to just about any business professional

There are no guarantees that retail businesses or restaurants or any other business entity will last forever, or that the business owner will be able to work his business forever. Competition, and changes in a marketplace, or one's health, can really destroy what had been a very viable business.

Recently, I needed to buy some lightbulbs. I went up the street to a store in my neighborhood that was a specialty lightbulb store. This store had every kind of a light bulb, and an ownership and staff that could answer any questions about lightbulbs. They were the light bulb store that catered to every kind of an entity that needed lightbulbs. People came from all over the city to find the right light bulb. When I drove up, I was shocked to find that their store was empty, and their space was for lease. Evidently, they could not compete with the big box stores that sell light bulbs much less expensively.

During hot days in the summer, and on nasty days during the rest of the year, my wife and I walk in a very popular mall. On weekdays, we are amazed at how little business the stores seem to be doing. This is very expensive retail space, and we often wonder how these stores stay in business. Regularly, we see tenant turnover, and sometimes even major tenant turnover. Articles are becoming more prevalent about malls becoming the "graveyard" of retail as we know it. This adds testimony to the idea that changes are happening faster than ever!

Everyone who is not independently wealthy needs the assurance of a backup, or second income that will outlast them. Currently, there are about eight million Americans who are working a second job just to make ends meet. These people are usually working for a low hourly rate that has no future. Their time would be much better spent, and their cash flow would be much greater, and their future much brighter, if they were building their own business. People need an affordable opportunity that will keep working for them, not a low hourly wage for which they will have to keep working!!

I had a good friend in the real estate business who asked an interesting question: Are you working for your business, or is your business working for you? The goal is to work for your business until it achieves a life of its own, at which time, it can start working for you!

Direct sales definitely offers that opportunity.

CHAPTER 25

CONSEQUENCES OF THE BIG FOUR

As individuals, and even as a country, we are likes corks in the ocean. Corks go where the ocean currents take them, without an option. Individuals and countries have some built in options, but there are some powerful currents that are impossible to reverse. These currents are called "trends."

I began Part II of this book by identifying these "Big Four" trends. I presented some examples of how these trends have led us to where we are today, and how these trends will influence our future.

There is one trend that is a serious national cancer that grows in a huge way every day. This cancer is known as the national debt. This cancer could kill our country's economy, and ruin everyone's financial future. This cancer needs to be treated and eliminated! This is one trend that can be reversed, but it will take a gigantic effort and a long time. The $20,000,000,000,000.00 debt wasn't borrowed overnight, and it won't be repaid overnight.

The other trends, such as longevity, technology, and a globalized economy have some very positive aspects, but even these positive trends are creating great challenges.

LONGEVITY

Longevity, as wonderful as it is, puts huge pressure on the healthcare industry and government entitlements. As people live longer, they become more susceptible to cancer, Parkinson's, heart disease, diabetes, and Alzheimer's Disease to mention only a few, and these conditions are outrageously expensive. Many experts believe that Alzheimer's Disease alone could bankrupt our healthcare system.

The other government entitlement that is negatively impacted by longevity is Social Security. Because of longevity, the government is going to need to pay Social Security to more people for a much longer period of time. Hey, I'm 80 years old, so I am a great proponent of longevity, but I also recognize that it comes with increasing economic challenges as this trend continues.

TECHNOLOGY

Technology is also a huge and powerful trend. It is absolutely mind boggling what the human race has been able to create and achieve. The benefits provided by technology, and the potential for future benefits is unlimited. But - and there is always a "but" - as we saw in a previous chapter, technology and automation, including robots, have eliminated and will continue to eliminate millions of jobs. I have heard recently that it is projected that in thirty years or sooner there will be no need for airline or military pilots. Drones will be doing their jobs.

The increase in globalization, an outgrowth of technology, is also a positive trend with some negative aspects. One positive is that because of international competition, we are able to negotiate great prices on imports from countries that have much lower overhead than we do, allowing American consumers to get the best prices in stores across the country. The other advantage is that globalization allows American companies, if they are competitive, to sell to the world.

We have also seen the negative results of globalization. Our country has not been able to compete in many areas of business, and as a result, we have lost millions of jobs and closed tens of thousands of factories in our country.

Devaluation of the dollar

Another powerful, disturbing and unstoppable trend is the dollar's loss of buying power. When I was in Italy in 1950, my family hired the owner of a sailboat to take us around the Isle of Capri. This was just five years after the end of World War Two, and the boat owner had just had the boat painted at a cost of ten thousand Lire. He had bought the boat before the war for a thousand Lire. The loss of purchasing power of the Lire, as a result of the war, happened very quickly and very visibly.

The dollar's loss of purchasing power is very much slower, but over the course of time, it has eroded in a huge way.

We have seen that in 1913, my father's part of the rent for his apartment in Manhattan in New York City was approximately eight cents a day. When I was a kid back in the 1940's, a penny would buy two pieces of Dubble Bubble gum with a separate cartoon printed in color. The proprietor who sold that gum was making a profit and appreciated the purchase! Today, I can't think of anything you can buy for a penny. In fact I can't think of anything you can buy for a nickel, a dime or a quarter!

Going back to the 1940s, you could buy a regular sized candy bar in a grocery store for as little as four cents, but they were known as "nickel candy bars". Today, in local grocery stores a nickel candy bar costs $1.59. This means that a dollar won't come close to buying a regular sized candy bar. A ten dollar bill will only buy six candy bars with a small amount of change, and a hundred dollar bill will only buy sixty two candy bars with some change.

Remember, back in 1950, my father bought me a Rolex with a hundred dollar bill, and got back twenty eight dollars. So you can easily see what is happening, and what will continue to happen on an even bigger scale. This trend grows by percentages, so as the numbers grow, the value of the dollar erodes even more quickly. This is the trend that killed my father's retirement savings.

On the basis of this, at current interest rates, saving money, over the long haul, is a losing proposition!

My advice is to acquire hard assets that will hold their value against the eroding dollar. Even better, acquire hard assets that will not only hold their value, but which will also throw off income based on the current value of the dollar.

Another powerful trend shown in this book is how major companies have had to change their compensation packages from being extremely protective of their employees by including terrific fringe benefits, to minimizing those benefits everywhere they can. Many great companies, over the course of time, became financially top heavy, and failed because of their unaffordable fringe benefits. This is the trend that our federal government is on with its entitlement programs. Don't allow yourself to expect help from an entity that won't be able to afford to help you.

It is easy to think that because the federal government is a taxing authority, there will always be tax dollars for entitlements. The problem is that the cash flow coming in from taxes at some point will, because of longevity and the health epidemics associated with it, and interest on the debt, not come close to supporting Social Security, Medicare, or any other government entitlements.

Turbulence in the job market is a developing trend that keeps growing. When I graduated from college in 1959, my classmates either went to graduate school, or applied for jobs. Many of us got multiple job offers, with decent starting salaries, and with an opportunity for upward mobility. It seemed that there were jobs for everyone. The unemployment rate was in the 5% range, but back then, that was regarded as full employment.

Today, we hear that students, even from the best schools, can't find work in their fields of study. As a result, they are having to move back in with their parents and work in low level, part time jobs, while looking for a meaningful full time opportunity.

Jobs are only offered at the pleasure of an employer. The employer is, usually, either an owner of the business, or a manager in the business. The only reason an employer would offer someone a job is because he or she believes that the person they are hiring would fill a need that would help the company make more money than it could make without the new employee. The employer is looking for employees who will enhance his or her income and make his or her department or company more financially successful.

Smart hiring gets managers promoted. Another part of smart hiring is to hire the best people at the lowest price the market will bear. When the job market is weak, the competition for jobs is strong, and prospective employees are forced to take what they can get. Additionally, in a weak market, current employees have a harder time earning salary increases.

In the recent Presidential election of 2016, job creation was the top concern of voters of both parties. The winner of the election, President Donald Trump, is committed to keeping jobs in America, bringing jobs back to America, and providing tax incentives to American corporations to encourage them to invest in building millions of new jobs in this country.

I think these are all great initiatives, and I applaud this effort. There is no doubt jobs are the backbone of the American work force. But -

and as I said, there is always a but - there is a finite number of jobs American corporations can afford to create, and jobs often end at age 65, if not before.

OUTSMARTING THE JOB TRAP

Here is a very important and powerful thought: In addition to encouraging job creation, let's also concentrate on creating new entrepreneurs. Entrepreneurs are the people in this country who create the most jobs, and many of these are high paying jobs. Even President Trump was an entrepreneur whose company created over twenty thousand jobs. It also made him a multi- billionaire.

Would you rather be an employer or an employee? I think the best answer to that question is: "I'd like to be both." Having a full time job is extremely important to most people, and jobs are usually very time consuming and demanding. Most people don't think they could be doing more.

But - once again, there is always a but - employees don't control their own destiny, and jobs usually don't last a lifetime. Job security in today's environment is at a very low level. Additionally, jobs are designed to make the ownership and top management rich, not most of the employees.

Consequently, employees must recognize the need to take control of their own destiny. The proper attitude today needs to be "my family and me first." If you don't put yourself first, no one else is going to. This is not being selfish; it is being smart, and it is being practical. Remember, this is the reality of the cold cruel world!

As an employee, the best way to put your family and yourself first is to start your own business while you are employed. As the founder of your business you need to find and create time to build this business. Your business has to be a priority right behind your family and your job.

The goal should be to build your business so big that you can no longer afford to keep your job. When this happens, you own your own life.

A SIMPLE PATH TO ENTREPRENEURSHIP

With this perspective in mind, a direct sales company fits the parameters perfectly. It has a very low entry fee, it requires no physical labor, it can be done in off hours, at the owner's leisure, and it can throw off unlimited rewards.

Additionally, it does exactly what our country is screaming for. As an entrepreneur, you have the opportunity to put volumes of people to work by putting them in business for themselves, and you have given them the same opportunity you have, which is to make an unlimited income. This can be a great answer the nation's jobs problem. Each successful entrepreneur could help create an unlimited income opportunity for an unlimited number of Americans.

A unique approach would be for an employer to offer his employee two ways to make money. The first way would be as an employee of the company, and secondly as an independent distributor in a direct sales company, sponsored by the employer. Not only could this create a long term, leveraged, residual income for the employee, it could do the same thing for the employer. In fact, the more employees, the better!

The Big Four are real, powerful, and unstoppable. In fact, they will continue to gain steam. It is your challenge to stay ahead of them. The 2016 election was won on the platform "America First" If each American takes a "me first" approach and builds a successful business, and helps others do the same, the country's tax base will pay off the national debt and fund our government's entitlement programs. We will all have contributed to making America great again, with no political bias.

Securing yourself financially is the first step to making that happen. My fervent hope is that my shot across the bow has given you the motivation you need to make sure your own ship sails long and free.

LET MY BOOK MAKE YOU MONEY!

The 100-year economic realities I've described in the preceding pages started with my father in 1913 and continued with me through 2016. As an author, I've made my best effort to be historically accurate. There is no bull strudel in my words.

As you absorb the message of the Hydeman story, it is important to understand that its emphasis is not on the past, but what the past tells us about the future. Unfortunately, it doesn't paint a very pretty picture looking ahead. There are very real challenges to be addressed!

As a reader, you have two choices: You can disbelieve what is depicted in this book, and do nothing about it, or you can believe what you have read and take action to protect your future.

As indicated earlier, this is not a book about HOW to do anything. The intent is to show WHY you need to take action, as well as WHEN to begin that action.

The WHEN should begin right now, with no procrastination!!

I brought up direct sales as a possible option because many of us don't know what we want to do, or could do. Direct sales companies are a prepackaged solution if you find one that meets your parameters. No matter your area of interest, there is a direct sales company that offers a product that dovetails with it. Health? Yes! Cosmetics? Yes! Travel? Yes! Food? Yes! Wine? Yes! Consumer products? Household goods? Yes! Business products? Yes! Legal Services? Yes! Jewelry? Yes! Technology? Yes! The list is endless; all you need to do is a little online research, or even ask your friends. If the process of building a business is more important than the product, there are numerous well-established companies that will be happy to talk to you and provide all the support in the world.

Something you need to expect in your direct sales business is the same thing that everyone in ANY kind of sales faces: a high percentage of rejection. The reason so many people fail in direct sales is that they can't stand rejection. They take rejection personally and feel very hurt by it. Rather than detach from the emotions, they quit and fail.

Your sponsor will happily provide all the support and mentoring you need to learn to overcome objections and deal with rejection. The best way to avoid rejection is to give your prospect solid reasons why they need the opportunity you are presenting to them. This book is loaded with those reasons!

If you like the idea of being an Independent Distributor in a direct sales company, use this book as a recruiting tool to explain to your prospects WHY they need to join your organization. Give this book to your prospects, and let them keep it when they join your team. Teach them to use it as a recruiting tool as well. Have enough books in the field at all times to increase your leverage and maximize your opportunity.

Your percentage of rejections will be dramatically reduced if your prospect understands how important your proposal is to his or her long term financial best interest and WHY he or she will benefit when they join you in building a business that can protect them for a lifetime.

I sincerely hope it helps protect your future and your retirement!

AFTERWORD

THE BEAT GOES ON

During the time this book was being written, our country had a presidential election. Republican candidate Donald Trump, to much of the country's amazement, defeated Democratic candidate Hillary Clinton to become our country's 45th president. President Trump succeeded President Barack Obama, a Democrat, and the new administration immediately began eliminating and replacing most, if not all, of the previous administration's initiatives that had been put in place by executive order, and the new president introduced his own agenda with volumes of his own executive orders.

Early in the Obama administration, the Democrats passed the Affordable Care Act, also known as Obamacare. They did this without a single Republican vote. The Republicans were, at that time, the party of resistance. It has since become apparent that Obama Care is failing, and the Republicans are intent on repealing, improving and replacing it. When, or if, this happens, it will probably be done without any Democrats voting for it. The Democrats have now become the strongly committed party of resistance!

During President Trump's first 100 days very little, if anything, was passed legislatively. He did get Justice Neil Gorsuch appointed to the Supreme Court, but it took the nuclear option to get that done.

Everything of political consequence is being done strictly on party lines, and there is no consensus on anything. The political divide is the worst in our country's history since the Civil War. The government is at a standstill on most important issues, and the American people are politically polarized to an extreme degree.

If our country is going to survive as we have known it, we, as a nation, have to come together. As John Dickinson, one of our founding fathers said back in 1768, "By uniting we stand, by dividing we fall." That statement is even truer today!

The fight over the healthcare bill is about making sure that as many people as possible get the coverage they need and can afford. The perfect solution, from a coverage standpoint would be Medicare for all, but from an affordability standpoint, it is absolutely unaffordable. Additionally, it is a Socialist solution, not a Free Enterprise solution. Frankly, even a Socialist or Communist government that was $20,000,000,000,000.00 in debt couldn't provide its citizens with satisfactory healthcare.

Neither political party could possibly come up with a universally acceptable healthcare plan that wouldn't drive our country much further into bankruptcy. This should not be viewed as a political problem. It needs to recognized as a huge American economic problem with no realistic fix. Common sense tells me that our government is way over its head regarding this issue with no, totally satisfactory, way out! Whichever party is in power at the time a healthcare bill gets approved will be blamed for its inadequacy or its failure.

Premiums and deductibles are going to have to continue to rise because of the loss of buying power of the dollar, and the government is going to have to raise the debt ceiling, which will accelerate inflation, and put even more pressure on taxpayers.

Every time our government gets involved in something, that something becomes much more complicated, and very much more expensive! The Big Four trends just keep picking up speed as they roll along. Last month the local grocery store raised the price of a regular sized candy bar from $1.59 to $1.79. In the foreseeable future, we could be looking at a $3.00 candy bar. Remember, when I was a kid, those same candy bars sold for as little as 4 cents!

Believe the numbers.
Healthcare costs, just like candy bars, will ride the trend
to much higher premiums and deductibles.

During this same 100-day time frame, Congress was faced with the challenge of agreeing on a bill to increase the debt ceiling in order to avert a government shutdown. Knowing they couldn't reach an agreement, they passed stopgap legislation that provided funding until September 30th, 2017, which is the end of the fiscal year. They didn't solve the problem. They just put it off into the future, at which time we may well experience a government shutdown.

This stopgap bill did include a significant increase in military spending, which our country desperately needs, because all the global hot spots are heating up. It is also indicative of the fact that our out-of-control federal debt will continue to spiral up. There is no end in sight to this unstoppable trend of National Debt. EBSA!

Yet again, it's clear that we must each take steps to protect ourselves financially by relying on our own ingenuity and drive, and not bet the farm on a company or on the government.

Sincerely,

Robert B. Hydeman
Dallas, TX
May 2017

ABOUT THE AUTHOR

Bob Hydeman was born in New York City in 1936. He graduated from The Hill School in 1955 and from Wesleyan University in 1959 with a B.A.

Bob's business experience includes being employed by several large public New York Stock Exchange companies, an American Stock Exchange company, a NASDAQ start-up, and, for twenty years, owning a commercial real estate brokerage company in Dallas, Texas.

Bob has been proudly married for over 54 years, to his best friend, and has two, terrific grown children and five spectacular grandchildren. This book is dedicated to them, their spouses and his sister.

Bob claims to have two goals in life, he has wanted to be rich and anonymous, and he brags that he achieved one of his goals at a very early age! He is still, in his old age, working on the other.